Philip Rawson

Sacred Tibet

136 illustrations, 18 in colour

Thames and Hudson

Contents

Introduction

The Plates   33

Themes   65

Introduction

The Buddhist art and culture of Tibet are unique in world history. The Chinese invasion of Tibet in 1950 and then the Chinese 'Cultural Revolution' of 1966–76 resulted in great massacres of people and monks, and the deliberate and massive destruction of art and monasteries; then in 1987–8 came further slaughter of Tibetans by the Chinese military authorities, determined to suppress demonstrations demanding independence. So the original epoch of religion and art in Tibet seems to have closed, and we can see its meaning entire. Refugee settlements in India and many Western countries, including Britain and the USA, now maintain and adapt the patterns of Tibetan life, teaching and art, and are gradually attracting more and more Western followers.

Its real interest for us is that Tibetan culture offers powerful, untarnished and coherent alternatives to Western egotistical lifestyles, our short attention span, our gradually more pointless pursuit of material satisfactions, and our despair when these, finally, inevitably, disappoint us. By Tibetan standards our arts seem to have a hollow centre, for they revolve around a theory of purely individual expression, regardless either of the spiritual stature of the person behind the expression or any value it may have for others. Our arts also aim to become both desire-stimulating commodities and investment stock; and, of course, have close links with advertising and entertainment. Such attitudes to art run exactly contrary to the values cherished by the Tibetan imagination, which inspires arts meant to be of specific use and spiritual benefit to everyone.

Growing numbers of people in the West are feeling a deep revulsion against the alternately brutal and subtle appeals to human cupidity on which so much of our culture is based. We realize how spiritually destructive these are; and we are forming resistance-groups to the crippling effects of our culture's materialism. Many of these groups follow Buddhist ideas. But where some artists and art-lovers may find the totally serene art from certain other Buddhist countries such as Thailand somewhat limited and remote, the Buddhist art and imagination of Tibet are full of brilliant stimuli to invention. If we explore the ideology and methods behind the art properly they can lead us far beyond merely appreciating the external appearance of original Tibetan work and enrich our lives immeasurably.

We do need to reach for the true content of Tibetan art, rather than weaving tissues of abstract thought around it. As André Malraux pointed out so vividly, major arts use their visual imagery to present what can *not* be seen, rather than reproducing everyday fact that can be seen. So, if we are to experience this art we need to enter as fully as possible into the region of meaning where the art itself moves, which is the subject of this book.

The Wheel of Existences, turned by the Great Power of Time. Above, sun and moon (with hare) as measures of cyclical time

Land of energies

Tibetan art is inspired by the need both to collaborate with and reconcile the violent energies expressed in the country's landscapes. Tibet has been called 'the Roof of the World'. Much of its chief plain is over fifteen thousand feet high, and ringed to the south by the world's highest mountains — the Himalayas — beyond them India; and to the north the great cold Kun-lun mountains, beyond them the vast Central Asian sand-deserts, windswept Mongolia and the immense Tsaidam swamps. To the west rears the Karakoram, across whose high, broken ranges lies Kashmir. Tibet's eastern margin breaks up into a multitude of enormous ridges and deep valleys through which emerge the rivers that water Southeast Asia: the Salween, the Mekong. Southwards flow the great rivers of India, the Brahmaputra (called in Tibet Tsangpo), the Indus and Sutlej. So Tibet is the source of much of southern Asia's water. Inside Tibet hundreds of lakes are fed by smaller rivers which do not escape through the ring of mountains. The land surface is sand and broken rock, with its own immense mountain ranges and sheer precipices. Icy dry winds sweep it continually. The capital city, Lhasa, at 11,830 feet rarely reaches a day temperature of 7 degrees C (45 degrees F) but can stay as low as minus 8 degrees C (18 degrees F). There is very little rain. The southwest monsoons which drench India cannot pass the Himalayan barrier: so the water which feeds those great rivers is virtually all snow-melt from the ranges of mountain peaks. Only in some of the deeper valleys, especially in the south-east, do any vigorous plant life or precious trees flourish in warmer temperatures. Elsewhere the permanent icy winds scour the landscape bare of trees.

Tibetan culture blends elements belonging to both the desert Tarim basin and windswept Mongolia to the north of the Kunlun range, and to baking, teeming India immediately south of the Himalayas. The northern sector is inhabited by nomads who live a high-altitude life in tents, not unlike that of the Mongol horse-breeders. The southern and western sectors have maintained their contacts across the mountains, especially with the kingdoms of Nepal, Bhutan, Sikkim and Kashmir which lie on the southern and western flanks of the Himalaya and Karakoram ranges. Because of the difficulty of the terrain and the ferocity of the inhabitants, the great land trade-routes of Asia which have existed since pre-Roman times skirted around the northern edge of the Kun-lun mountains, crossing the Tarim basin and Inner Mongolia, by-passing Tibet entirely.

This formidable and secret country has depended for much of its food and most of its transport upon the animal called the yak, a long-haired ox. Cross-bred with the cow, the yak gives good milk and high-fat butter which is burned in thousands of temple lamps. It grows extra-long hair to resist the permanent icy cold. As well as the yak, long-haired sheep provide both wool for weaving and the sheepskin clothing which Tibetan people wear fleece inward, belted against their skin, often slipping one arm out of its long sleeve to do their jobs.

The food of Buddhist Tibetans is not basically vegetarian, although they do not hunt animals for food. Roast barley meal (*tsampa*), butter, cheese, and meat of yak and sheep (which may be dried) are staples. In the dry, cold climate it keeps for a long time. Rice is a rare luxury. People drink gallons of tea, imported from China, mixed with salt and yak butter. They grow garden vegetables and eat some wild plants, such as the nettle that has kept hermits

A provincial fortress, a typically multi-level and multi-storey building perched over a rocky precipice

alive. Fruit and nuts do grow and ripen in the warmer valleys, but are not easy to get.

This desperately taxing terrain has bred an exceptionally tough and intelligent population living a hardy life at high altitude. They are ethnically kin to the Mongols and some Chinese; their Tibetan language is related to the Burmese spoken by the tribal peoples who infiltrated and conquered Burma from the north during the ninth to fifteenth centuries AD. Both groups speak languages called 'Tibeto-Burman'.

Before they adopted Buddhism fully between about AD 650 and 900 the Tibetans were violently quarrelsome and turbulent. Tibetan society was at bottom feudal. Chieftains and kings have dominated and fought over the different regions. Craftsmen, farmers and agricultural peasantry have lived normal hard lives. But Buddhism brought its monasteries as centres of art and scholarship, patronized by the rulers, to which almost every family sent a son or daughter. This introduced a completely new factor into the social system which radically affected its structure. It enabled the humblest person to attain very high standing by merit alone. The modern Chinese Maoist invaders found the system incomprehensible, since it did not fit their *a-priori* social theory. They could only interpret the monasteries as feudal agencies of oppression, which their own version of Marxist dogma obliged them to obliterate.

Tibetans have always felt their environment as an arena of energies, and themselves as inwardly constituted of similar energies. So they carried on all aspects of their lives including their religion vigorously, alternating sustained strenuous physical effort with relaxation and laughter. They did not simply struggle against their environment, but developed techniques for enlisting its energies, both physical and metaphysical. The version of Buddhism they adopted personified and systematized both outer and inner energies; and its disciplines were felt to have material as well as spiritual effects.

The shamanic base

Before Buddhism arrived and spread across Tibet the people's spiritual vigour had been expressed in their shamanic form of religion, called *Bön-po*. Such a form seems to have been fundamental in archaic societies the world over, including Asia, Europe and America. In Tibet as elsewhere, shamanic rites and mythology incorporated powerful and noble symbols and imagery. A century ago, westerners used to call shamans 'witch doctors' because one of their functions in their societies was to heal the sick, usually by means of impressive public dance-rituals using symbolic objects. The shaman is a man or woman who has access to the world of the dead, of spirits and divine beings. He or she becomes a shaman by experiencing a 'call', enduring a profound sickness, and dying to their ordinary personality. During a period of solitary endurance in the forest or desert, he or she is visited and initiated by spirits, and meets a particular spirit who will be the contact in the spirit world.

All conceptions of spirit are based on an idea about the dead, the ancestors. Archaic peoples recognized that when someone dies, their eyes close, their blood stills, they stop breathing and an invisible something seems to leave their bodies, which then become mere residues of flesh, bone, hair and nails. So an equation emerges: the living body minus the dead

The embodiment of air: Garuḍa, golden feathered sun-bird of heaven and dominator of earthly snake-energies

body equals a factor identified as a life-energy which has left the corpse to inhabit another region beyond the present world. Most often they identify this energy with the vital breath, whose realm is the air (the English word 'spirit' comes from Latin word *spiritus* meaning wind and breath), but sometimes also with the blood and other bodily fluids. This spirit vitalizes the body and is passed on in procreating children. It is the principal force inspiring art, and the overwhelming majority of works of so-called 'primitive' art are meant to give it visible body and shape. Open, watching eyes are its principal sign, along with exotic head-shapes and sometimes bodies in vigorous and formal dance-movement. Shamans wear special headgear and costumes to execute their dances, during which they may be possessed by spirits.

Like other archaic peoples the pre-Buddhist Tibetans interpreted the forces of the outer world in terms of their own spiritual life-energy. They saw the objects of nature — trees, rocks, mountains, lakes — not as inert but animate, and interpreted them as manifesting spirits of their own far more powerful than humans and capable of destroying them totally. They visualized these spirits as enormous, dangerous and savage beings shaped like humans but equipped with great fangs, lolling tongues, vast arms, huge bellies and florid sexual organs who love to feed on the flesh of living creatures and drink their life-blood. So, in pure shamanic rituals, the sacrifice of animals or even of people played an important part. When Buddhism came to Tibet shamanic rituals did not vanish, though their bloody sacrifices were reinterpreted as metaphorical. Buddhist monks and nuns took over many of the shaman's rites, myths and symbolisms, and adapted them to Buddhist ideas.

Normally spirits are invisible, and in Tibet they inhabit high places and move freely in the moving air (the region of 'life-breath'). So art may represent them with wings. And shamans who are on familiar terms with them wear costumes decorated with bird-feathers or beaks ('feathered skirts and rainbow jackets'), use implements which move the air rhythmically to produce sound, such as trumpets or drums, and wear floating scarves that curl in the wind.

In Tibet the equipment original shamans used to contact and control spirits was often made of human bone for the sake of its supernatural power, and Tibetan Buddhist magicians wore aprons and ornaments made up of carved fragments of bone, blew trumpets made from human thigh-bones and beat drums made from human skulls and skin. When Buddhism in Tibet 2–3, 6–8 took over the old Bön-po cult of spiritual powers and magical energy, it re-interpreted the shamanic conceptions in Buddhist terms.

The wonderful archaic myths preserved in Bön-po shamanism imagine a source of creation, a beginning of things, long 'before' or 'behind' the degenerative entropy-processes of decay which are brought about by passing time and the distracting busyness of everyday actuality. As Mircea Eliade has often pointed out, archaic rituals for sending off the dead, for seasonal renewal, for healing people from disease, or for changing an unpleasant course of historical events carry the people who participate out of their present, 'back' to an 'original' condition, an archetypal order. This cancels out what is wrong with the present, gives the community a fresh start by setting going a fresh re-ordered creation. For this reason the arrival of the Buddha's religion was felt to initiate a kind of ultra-shamanism. Though it recognized spiritual entities to be ultimately no less illusory than any other level of 'reality', Tibetan Buddhism's world is spiritual.

The arrival of Buddhism

Buddhism was founded during the sixth century BC by a prince called Gautama who lived in northern India. He married and had a son but then left home in response to a call and became a homeless, wandering ascetic. After trying out and rejecting the extremes of asceticism he took to his own 'Middle Way' and became, at length, Buddha, 'awoken' or 'enlightened'. Eventually he attained Nirvana, the 'blowing out' of the flame of cravings and delusions. He spent the rest of his life building up his begging order of monks and nuns and organizing its rule of life. He preached continually to them and to lay people, wandering around the great cities which then flourished in the middle Ganges valley. He died, aged about eighty, passing into Pari- (complete) Nirvana; which meant he would never again be 'reborn'. His teaching spread into every region of Asia, never imposing itself by force, but taking its place as the pinnacle of whatever religion was already there.

Buddhism developed many different strands of practice and philosophy in many different countries. All however are based on the same fundamental doctrines, and all agree in rejecting any idea of, or statement about, a named God; not because they do not know an Ultimate, but because they refuse to define it or speak about it, on the assumption that to do either is to mislead and limit. Only direct experience of the Ultimate really matters. Individuals may reach it by following certain practical methods. That is all. These methods are the substance of Buddhism. They may sound easy, but they are not. Normal individuals can only fulfil them after many lifetimes of sustained effort. For Buddhists accept the ancient Indian notion of continuous reincarnation through successive lifetimes, as part of method. But the deeper Buddhist doctrines about ultimate reality beyond time show the idea of a simple succession of many lives as animal and human in historical time to be ultimately naïve. Already before AD 400, the classic *Lotus sutra* had developed the intuition that the universe is unknowably vast, containing millions upon millions of cosmoses and worlds 'numberless as the sand-grains of the Ganges river', all continuously arising from and falling back into an indefinable Ultimate. It is into this context that we have to set the image of reincarnation that is part of Buddhist teaching.

Buddhism consists purely of techniques for wiping away the behavioural and mental 'stains' which restrict or block our clear insight. This insight may either dawn gradually on us or arrive suddenly. It is in fact nothing but the natural condition of the integrated clear mind, which appears only when desires, longings, beliefs, habits and false perceptions that arise from attachment and clinging to things are stripped away.

On the face of it Buddhism offers us negative incentives: every major Buddhist sermon or text contains somewhere in its early passages the phrase 'Everything is suffering'. This really means that everything we hold to is an obstacle to the clear mind; so personal release depends on developing indifference to desire and hate. Buddhists commit themselves to a tremendous many-lives-long process of mental and physical discipline and meditation. The Buddha refused to name or describe any ultimate goal

Atisa, founder of the Kandampa sect, displaying from his heart the Bodhisattva Manjūśrī of whom he was an incarnation

A Sakyapa-sect teacher

save release from the suffering caused by attachment to self-identity. He pointed out that all things are transient and vanishing. However firmly based, delightful and happy they may seem at any moment, their passing causes endless grief, so the only right and sensible course is to escape from the world-cycles (*Saṁsāra*) as urgently as from a burning building.

To unfasten the grip of *Saṁsāra* is to attain Nirvana as the Buddha did, when the impulses that drive us on to further incarnations, based on attachment to the world and longing for life, are snuffed out. The awoken person is no more reborn, and escapes totally from the cycles.

The methods for reaching Nirvana are based on continuous introspective mindfulness, physical and mental control and self-criticism. You develop a permanent watchfulness over what you do, say, think and feel. You check unflinchingly the endlessly rolling inner cinema film of shameful images, deluding, often frantic urges, fears and bitter egotistic resentments which normally occupy your mind. You should learn to examine them all dispassionately, with a tranquil mind, as if watching a river flow past, and realize them as hollow and unreal. You can only do this by developing the capacity for prolonged introspective concentration, and the ability to ignore distractions of every kind. To succeed in all this you need the right equipment, called generically 'means' or 'method'.

Some people may feel that this process is unduly negative, rejecting as valueless all experience and phenomena. But that negative is itself an illusion. Buddhists need to counter illusory beliefs one by one in order to reach the ultimate reality beyond names and categories.

Images for the transcendent

Buddhism has terms for a number of central realizations we need to experience. We can only grasp the meaning of the terms if we try to attain those realizations ourselves. The terms are given here in Sanskrit and translated into English, but no English words can carry their full Buddhist meanings. Tibetan art is entirely devoted to inducing these realizations, and its figurative imagery always refers to them.

The terms are: *Anātmatā*, meaning non-selfhood, the absence of limiting self-identity in people and things; *Śūnya*, Void or emptiness; *Dharma*, literally support, essence of the teaching, Buddhist practice; *Skandhas*, the groups or categories of experience; *Karma*, the set of deeds performed through the whole series of individual lifetimes; *Puṅya*, merit so gained; *Prajñā*, wisdom; and *Upāya*, 'skilful means'.

Anātmatā cancels the conventional idea that the world is made up of independent entities, each entity or 'self' having its own inherent existence, apart from our perceptions and imputation of names. We need to go beyond the self-centred world view that falsely interprets the reality we experience as a collection of separate lumps of 'thing' impinging on ourselves, defined by concepts and words, on which 'we ourselves' can 'act', and about whose relationships 'we' can 'calculate' and 'philosophize'. (*Calculus* in Latin means 'a little pebble'.) The imagery of beings and things of Buddhist arts is never more than provisional, useful to help people still caught in the trap of a world of objects which they either desire or hate – both of which feelings constitute attachment – and from which as Buddhists we desire urgently to escape. We resolve all oppositions, definitions and contrasts of feeling and belief in following the Buddha's way.

Once we loosen our attachments to separate things we begin to be at a loss to talk about what it is we are realizing. Though we can call it 'no-*thing*-ness', it is *not* nothingness. The luminous totality we come to know has no separable things or oppositions in it since every appearance is a function of all others.

Buddhists call this *Śūnya*, the 'Void', emptiness — a negation of our ignorant perceptions of ourselves and things as independent entities. It includes, and so reaches far beyond, all the thoughts about 'reality' that our brains can formulate. So it is hyper-cosmic. It can generate, as apparitions in itself, powers, worlds, cosmoses and vast aeons of time, all of which display only something of its potential.

At the ordinary human level, to begin to reach any experience of the Void we need first of all to find ways of getting rid of those delusory identifications and attachments to distinct things that confine us like prison bars into our banal everyday reality. One potent metaphor for the Void, often used in Tibetan art, is the sky. As the sky is the emptiness that offers clouds to our perception, so the Void is the 'space' in which objects appear to us in response to our attachments and longings. The Buddhist figures which Tibetan art represents are explained as 'explosions from the Void'. And the sky with its clouds so often represented as the background to figures in Tibetan 'hanging paintings', Tankas, symbolizes that Void from which all the figures are apparitions.

28, 38

Dharma means generically 'support'. Used in the singular as in 'the Buddhist Dharma', it means the Path, the teaching and practices which support the Buddhist life. But it also means those strands of mental and sensuous activity which appear and disappear constantly as we move about and live, and which we wrongly take as having those cores of substantial identity we attribute to 'things' and 'people'. They are all transient, flickering by quickly or slowly, sometimes instantaneously; and if we do think they are produced by constant identities because they seem repeatable, we misinterpret what we are perceiving and handicap ourselves for going on to recognize the infinitely luminous Void. Buddhism calls false identifications 'stains' or 'impurities' on the clear mind produced by those desires and hates we normally cherish and live by.

The *Skandhas*, literally 'heaps', are the five categories of experience from which we normally construct the illusory cores to Dharmas; and 'questioning them' forms the basis for all Buddhist meditational practice, which we should try to continue even during ordinary everyday life. Looking inward, we can catch each of the Skandhas in turn working in our mental and physical life to delude us. Questioning them one by one, analyzing every experience in terms of them, we come to realize that they have no 'objective core', and that if we go on believing and acting as though they have, we will never experience the comprehensive Void.

The five Skandhas are: name and form (Sanskrit *nāma-rūpa*, Tibetan *gzugs*); feelings or emotions (*vedanā* or *tshor-ba*); perception or recognition of phenomena (*samjñā* or *hdu-shes*); consciousness, the matching and classifying of 'things' intellectually to form mental structures (*visjñāna* or *nam-par-shes-pa*); constituting factors (Sanskrit *vāsanā* or *samskāra*, Tibetan *hdu-byed*. One of the Skandhas is symbolically associated with each of the five Dhyāni Buddhas visualized in meditation using mandalas (see p. 29).

Karma is the totality of what we each choose to do and think during all our lives. It develops progressively, through successive lifetimes, and its quality depends on the quality of our acts of body, speech and mind, and governs our success in eventually awakening from Saṃsāra. Only our own efforts can save us. Poor or bad Karma keeps us shut into the treadmill of dismal lifetimes and the cycle of suffering (often called the Wheel of Existences, and depicted repeatedly in Tibetan art).

Good Karma, based on moral behaviour, right action and developing consciousness of Skandhas, tots up as *Punya*, merit; and Punya can gradually prise us free from the cycles of suffering by producing for us ever more advantageous births. This is why the Buddha and saints were portrayed as high-born and princely. Their advantageous life-status reflected their merit-status. It is good Karma that leads a person to become a monk or nun.

Prajñā is the awareness which discriminates between false or deceptive reality and ultimate reality, the wisdom which perceives the emptiness of all conceptions, projections and contradictions. 'Form is emptiness, emptiness is form'. There is a set of basic texts called the *Prajñā Pāramitā*, a name which means broadly, the 'All-transcending Wisdom'. They are devoted to demonstrating that every positive and negative assertion, however subtly imagined, is equally empty of final truth. So in Tibetan art a set of books, perhaps balanced on a lotus flower, may symbolize pure Wisdom. Many female figures in Tibetan art personify Wisdom in its various stages.

36
25–6

Personification is very important in the whole imaginative and artistic complex of Tibet. In the earliest Buddhist art of India, between about 200 BC and AD 200, it was felt that to represent the Buddha in ordinary human form was wrong. The fact that he had attained Nirvana implied that he had passed beyond the limits of humanity. So simple objects were used to signify his presence in the many sculptural reliefs representing events in which he had taken part: a cushion on his seat, a pair of lotus-marked footprints, or the archaic symbol of a fiery pillar. But by the first century AD Indian images of the Buddha had begun to be carved and painted.

The three bodies

Through the early centuries AD Buddhist thinkers developed a range of images to meet people's need to visualize the Buddha, around which they could focus their thoughts and feelings. These images were based on a doctrine that the Buddha has three bodies (*Trikāya*). Both the doctrine and the art it justifies are meant as *Upāya* or 'skilful means' for leading peoples' minds gradually out of their selfish obsessions with worldly things towards concentrating on the Buddhist goal, to be abandoned once the goal is reached. 'Skilful means' include both personal practice and outward teaching. To divert yourself or others from pursuing worldly concerns, or from constructing merely intellectual systems that fascinate the mind, is excessively difficult. So through the centuries Buddhism developed its range of figurative imagery to symbolize the Buddhist goal. This imagery was expressly designed to enlist and focus our human faculties and emotions, including those that are normally damaging.

The doctrine of the three bodies of the Buddha resolves several philosophical and artistic problems at once. All three are supposed to be in some sense congruent. The first body, the *Nirmāṇakāya*, is the physical or manifest dimension of existence, represented by the Buddha Gautama and successive incarnations and embodiments of Buddhahood. The third body, called the Dharmakāya, is the Enlightened or Buddha mind, and became identified with the total body of true Enlightenment and doctrine, encompassing Dharma, all existence and phenomena, selflessness, wisdom, Void. The Dharmakāya is invisible and cannot be encompassed in thought.

Between these two bodies is the second, the Body of Glory, *Sambhogakāya*, an 'ideal' body composed of symbolic, not merely anatomical attributes. As the Sva-Sambhoghakāya, visionary, 'extremely perfect, pure, eternal and universal', it can only be seen by Bodhisattvas and people of a very high degree of insight; as Parasambhoghakāya, 'the body that causes enjoyment to others', it has thirty-two symbolic marks, and it is these attributes that usually provide a basis for the 'Buddha-image' depicted in art. It is inwardly 'void', a hollow continuum, smoothly rounded and golden-coloured, with long arms that are shaped like the trunks of elephants. It has lotus-roundels on palms of hands and soles of feet, a bump on the crown of the head, hair in short 'snail-shell' curls (the Buddha cut his hair with his sword as his first act of renunciation), and the sexual organs covered with a membrane. It is as colossal as imagination and art can make it, since it is meant to embrace everything that is. The conception of Sambhogakāya is implicit in many figures of Buddhist iconography.

To their normally illiterate audiences Buddhist monks used to recite Buddhist stories and doctrinal texts in the preaching halls of shrines, usually seated beneath images with the marks of the Sambhogakāya. This indicated that they were speaking, not simply on behalf of themselves, or even of the earthly Buddha, but of the Dharmakāya — the Buddha-mind.

Just as no icon of the Buddha was ever meant to represent his physical likeness, to be 'appreciated' externally, so all other figures of Buddhist iconography are meant to be understood in a special symbolic sense. Each invites the viewer, as he or she intently contemplates it, to identify with it — to absorb not the stone or painted image as such, but the state and stage of personal development to which its characteristic features refer. These features are explained in doctrinal texts. So the many varied icons represented in Tibetan art are not meant to depict separate objective or imaginary human-shaped beings, or even particular spirit-beings, but states of being which the human viewer is meant inwardly to adopt. To achieve this everyone needs to carry out long, continuous, often repeated acts of dedication and concentration. This constitutes the central activity of the Tibetan Buddhist monk or nun, which monastic rituals, recitations, music and art are all meant to help along.

We should therefore think of all Buddha figures and all the other figures in Buddhist art, including the sexual pairs, as archetypes: not in the Jungian sense, but more literally as high prototypes, ever more inclusive patterns of the Dharma-conscious person. Every monk, every visitor or member of a Buddhist audience, contemplates every image as showing a spiritual condition to which he or she can personally aspire and expect to reach one day, maybe millennia into the future.

Tibetan art does sometimes present images of individuals known to history, notably the founders of two of the main lines of teaching, 29 Padmasambhava and Tsongkapa, as well as other saints such as Milarepa,

18 and sainted kings. Tibetan Buddhism also accepts the doctrine of the *Tulku*. Tulkus are reincarnations of abbots and teachers who are looked on as special Buddhist archetypes, incarnate for a while in human form. Individuals who reach a stage of almost-Buddha, using their stock of merit entirely for their own Enlightenment, are called *Arhats*. The Buddha's first immediate disciples were the first historical Arhats. In China, which always prefers the individual instance to the general type, Arhats, known as *Lohan*, were very popular subjects for art, and they are sometimes also represented in Tibetan art. But later Buddhism tended to look on such people as selfish, and to prefer the ideal of the universally compassionate Bodhisattva.

Bodhisattvas

One of the most important attributes every practising Buddhist cultivates is kindliness, which when pushed to the limit develops into total compassion. In this, Buddhism is almost unique among the world's religions: only Jainism matches it. Every competitive aggression or grabbing, every desire or disgust, every dogmatic assertion, sets up conflicts which can only obscure the Void. The moment you say 'I believe so and so' you reduce or affront someone else, set up a conflict and so impede realization. For this reason most Bodhisattva figures of Buddhist art wear soft, kindly expressions, displaying the Universal Compassion for suffering creatures that was the reason for the Buddha's own life and teaching. At one level total kindliness simply means avoiding all hatred and partiality towards individuals. But in its broadest aspect it means seeing every suffering and struggling being, at whatever stage of its evolution, and however unwholesome it may seem, as calling for the total compassion of *Bodhicitta*, 'awakening mind'. This may require from the compassionate one all sorts of activity, some even seeming superficially unethical, aimed at leading particular beings towards their ultimate release. The Bodhisattvas are the archetypal personifications of such total compassion and of metaphysical insight. One of the most 36 popular is named in Sanskrit Avalokiteśvara, the 'Looking-down Lord'. He is called Kuan-yin in Chinese, and Chen-re-zi in Tibetan. Each Dalai Lama, the spiritual ruler of Tibet, originally residing in the capital, Lhasa, is held to be a fresh incarnation of Chen-re-zi.

The Bodhisattva figure represents the last human stage before total Enlightenment of a Buddha-to-be and his attainment of the Dharmakāya. Our earthly Buddha was referred to as 'the Bodhisattva' before he attained Enlightenment, since it was compassion for the universe of suffering that impelled him in the first place to undertake the intense discipline and meditation which led him to his ultimate insight, and hence to his ability to offer others guidance towards their own release.

There are many stories about the Buddha's previous lives, during which he cultivated earlier versions of the total compassion which helped lead him to Enlightenment. One recounts how as a young prince he was walking in his estate one day when he came across a tigress who had a broken leg, and so could not feed her cubs. She was lying under a high rock. The prince climbed to the top of the rock and flung himself down beside her, so that she could eat his flesh.

The Bodhisattva becomes such by dedicating all the vast store of merit-energy he or she has accumulated over millennia and myriads of incarnations towards the release of all suffering beings who are still struggling in the cycles of delusions. Individuals can call on particular Bodhisattvas for help, and they may appear by force of magic in a whole variety of different shapes on different occasions, including those of saviours and prophets. Art does not simply *portray* Buddhas and Bodhisattvas, but is meant to bring them into physical presence. The Bodhisattva-image particularly brings seemingly remote and difficult doctrine into direct touch with the hopes and fears of ordinary people, and meets their spiritual needs. There are many legends about their deeds of compassion.

In spirit-haunted Tibet, Buddhist figures in art may also embody supernatural and terrifying magical power. Whereas in most other Buddhist art the images express only kindness and gentle compassion, in Tibetan art all may be shown wearing 'furious', energetic aspects which express the supernatural power of their redirected merit-energy. Though their acts may genuinely be working for the ultimate salvation of beings, they may seem anything but kind and gentle to a particular being at a particular time. Such figures can even appear hostile or wicked, because their ultimately benevolent effects are only visible to the long-range insight of the Bodhisattva.

Energies of mantra and vajra

Personification is one principal way of representing and embodying energies, but they are also conveyed in more abstract terms that came to Tibet from the regions of north-eastern India and Kashmir, where a special version of Buddhism was flourishing by AD 600. This version shared the fundamental beliefs and texts common to all Buddhists but conveyed them in its own specific ways. It is usually called Mantrayāṇa or Vajrayāṇa. 'Mantrayāṇa' means 'the way of mantras' (or power-invocations); 'Vajra-yāṇa', 'the way of Vajra', denotes harnessed cosmic energy and mind. Mantrayāṇa-Vajrayāṇa amounts to the most comprehensive elaboration and combination of Buddhist thought we know.

Power-syllables – mantras – have been used in all Indian religions from ancient times, but in Mantrayāṇa Buddhism they were specially important. Such syllables or strings of syllables concentrate specific energies; and when someone utters them correctly they can induce the presence, both inwardly and outwardly, of those energies. In Mantrayāṇa the energies are usually also visualized as beings in human shape who personify the subtle components of Buddhist teaching. There are hundreds of them. Many works of figural art are inscribed with mantras, reciting which brings the 'presence' of the figures represented into their images for ritual or meditation. Tibetan art exists specifically to provide dwellings for spiritual principles representing inner states.

'Vajra', *dorje* in Tibetan, means both 'thunderbolt' and 'diamond', two metaphors for the energy of the Void in which all opposites are reconciled. It also refers symbolically to the erect male sexual organ. The shape of the *dorje* seems to be derived from an ancient power-emblem shaped like the thunderbolt that classical Zeus is sometimes represented hurling. The thunderbolt or lightning-strike is a universal and natural symbol for concentrated energy, while the diamond is the hardest and most brilliant of stones, interpreted as the crystal form of pure light. Several of the ritual implements used in Tibet have hilts shaped like thunderbolts. The *phur-bu* is a dagger with a triangular blade and a *dorje*-hilt. The monk-magician uses it

The vajra and its unfolding energies

15

during his rituals to control and compel dangerous spiritual energies. It is
also the physical embodiment of the mantra of the Buddha-mind, *Hūṁ*.

Perhaps the most famous of all mantras in Tibet is one that is chanted thousands of times a day and by virtually the entire population. It is inscribed on rocks and buildings, on clothes and the charms many people wear. It runs: *Oṁ maṇi padme Hūṁ*. The syllable *Oṁ* is a very ancient Indian invocation of the Supreme Reality; *maṇi* means 'jewel' or 'diamond' in Sanskrit, the diamond of vajra; *padme* means 'in the lotus'; *Hūṁ*, like the *phur-bu*, invokes energetic power.

To recite *Oṁ maṇi padme Hūṁ* invokes the archetypal presence of the vitalizing powers of creation, and amounts to an incantation for restoring the 'original' pure condition of the world. It is therefore an extremely powerful action to recite it, and people do so as many times during their lives as they can. It has many layers of symbolic reference. The first and last syllables are general. But *maṇi padme*, 'jewel in the lotus', has a deep doctrinal background in the Indian symbol-system which interprets ideas so ancient that they seem timeless.

The lotus, *padma*, has a complex of profound references. The water-borne lotus grows up from the invisible depths of bottom-mud to open and flower in the air. The opening blossom is an analogy for any process which involves crossing the boundaries between orders of experience, especially from the invisible to the visible. In the East, the emerging bud and opening lotus became a prime image for the appearance of developing regions which spring from an invisible 'beyond'. The manifest world is the 'lotus realm'. Buddhas and Bodhisattvas are represented in Tibetan art as borne into 'the visible' sitting or standing on lotus flowers.

The lotus also has an ancient traditional reference to the female genital organs, specifically to the genital organ of the Goddess who gives birth to the world ('Genesis'), and in the Buddhist context, to spiritual insight into the appearance and disappearance of phenomena.

Maṇi refers to that jewel of light, the condensed vajra-energy, as fertilizing like a drop of transcendent semen the lotus realm. Without it, no world could be born, nor any enlightenment attained. *Oṁ maṇi padme Hūṁ* invokes, every time it is uttered, the presence of the Ultimate Power which is at the very root of manifest creation, and so re-awakens the pristine condition.

A fundamental image cherished by all the Central Asian peoples living in their vast and barren terrain was the Paradise Garden. Buddhism adopted it also, as a way of engaging the fears and hopes of ordinary people, interpreting it as a Western Paradise. It is conceived and represented in art as a beautifully laid-out, flower-filled garden, its trees laced with strings of jewels, its ponds and lakes filled with gleaming precious stones. This image was described in major early texts as belonging to the realm of the Buddha Amitāyus, which means 'limitless life'. Anyone who earnestly calls on the name of Amitāyus, as he or she dies, may be born into the sunset realm from the bud of a lotus flower that rises from the surface of one of the lakes, into the presence of the Buddha. From 'there' — not a place but a blissful spiritual condition — it is easy to reach ultimate salvation. The paradisal idea is a very important ingredient in the imagination behind Tibetan imagery with its planned layouts and flowery, jewel-strung ambience.

Buddha Amitāyus-Amitābhā of the Western Paradise with immortality-nectar vase, seated on a lotus

Religious life and arts

The Buddhism and arts of Tibet are versions of those taken over intact and wholesale, partly via Kashmir, but mainly direct from north-eastern India between the seventh and tenth centuries AD, when that region was ruled by the Pāla kings. In Tibet they were moulded into characteristically Tibetan forms. Under the new influence its whole culture was radically altered and Tibet became a relatively peaceful country, focused intensely on its religion and art.

In Pāla north-east India, a group of enormous Buddhist monastery-universities flourished until they were totally destroyed by the Muslims who conquered the region early in the twelfth century, forcing monks to flee for refuge to Tibet. The sites of some are known; Nālandā has been carefully excavated. Others at Vikramaśīla and Odantapuri have been studied. They contained huge libraries of Sanskrit texts and were staffed by scholars who taught specialized courses not only religious but also secular, for example engineering and hydraulics. Versions of the texts survive in a huge number of scattered Sanskrit manuscripts, only some of which have so far been studied by modern Indian and Western scholars. Now that Tibetan monks have once again been driven from their home to other countries, they are bringing with them and recopying their sacred texts.

Buddhism came to Tibet along with a huge body of this Sanskrit literature which Tibetan scholars translated and copied repeatedly down the centuries. The texts were classified into two main groups, *the Kanjur*, 'word of the Buddha', containing the discourses of the Buddha and root-texts of the *Tantras*, and the *Tanjur* containing extensive commentaries by the masters. Both are preserved in monastic libraries. The live traditions too were carried to Tibet by immigrant or refugee Indian masters, or by Tibetans who went to India to study. A very beautiful Tibetan script was developed, based on the Indian Sanskrit Nāgarī, which as carrier of the doctrine was felt to have a sacred force of its own. The Chinese technique of wood-block printing on paper was adopted quite early to print editions of the texts; and both manuscripts and prints were often illustrated. Book pages were separate long horizontals, stacked and wrapped in cloth, kept between wooden boards carved with figures and foliage. The books were themselves revered as containers of wisdom.

The layout of the original Tibetan monastery was based upon the Indian monastery-university. All Indian Buddhist monasteries consisted of shrines and teaching halls surround by living-cells. Tibetan monasteries were similar in principle but their architecture was distinctive, adapted to Tibet's violent landscape and constant wind and cold. They were tall, multi-storeyed *15, 16* structures often perched towering over great rock-precipices, looking out *21* across wide terrain. They contained halls for communal ceremonies, regular worship and teaching, as well as storeys of cells for the community of monks or nuns. These people wore dark-red woollen robes and lived according to specific rules first laid down by the Buddha himself. They came from many social backgrounds, since it was conventional for most families to send at least one child to the 'best' monastery they could, for the spiritual benefit of both child and family. Some sects permitted monks co-habitation and life outside the monastery, but most did not. Monks could work as farmers or traders either inside or outside, a custom which is helping them to adapt to the circumstances of their life in new homes.

Monk walled up in a rock cell for years-long meditation, holding out his recitation rosary

Tibetan monasteries might be large or small; under the protection of powerful aristocrats they could grow to huge proportions, containing many hundreds of monks. The abbots of the chief monasteries were powerful figures, seen as incarnations of transcendent principles. On the death of one such abbot, his successor had to be his specific reincarnation (*Tulku*) who needed to be discovered by a committee from the monastery, which could take many years in searching. They might travel thousands of miles tracking down the one boy who was able to pick out the dead abbot's possessions from a random collection of objects.

Monasteries focused, as all Buddhist institutions do, on a symbolic architectural structure called in India *stupa*, in south-east Asia *dagoba* or *pagoda*, in Tibet *chörten*. It consists of a set of diminishing square and circular tiers carrying a round dome, which is crowned by a spire. Originally in India the stupa had been a reliquary-monument containing fragments of the cremated body of the Buddha or of one of his saints, but it quickly became a pure embodiment of the idea of Parinirvana. Its tiers were interpreted as the five Elements or *Dhātus*. The Dhātus range upwards, from dense to subtle: Earth, Water, Fire, Air, and Mind or total Consciousness. At Gyantse, for example, the chief chörten is very large and contains circuits of cell-shrines, but hundreds of small solid versions were stone-built all over the wild Tibetan countryside, and it was also employed as a graphic symbol. It is an emblem of Dharmakāya, source and goal of the phenomenal world.

The idea of the altar also came to Tibet from India. It represents a centre or 'terminal' where the power of the holy embodied in the chörten emerges to show itself, and where it can be invoked by ritual for the benefit of the community or the individual. Some shrines are specific to a place, their altar images representing local spirits or famous saints, but the images presiding over Buddhist altars normally represent the principal persons of the Buddhist spiritual hierarchy. Monasteries usually contained several altars, ranging from large communal ones in the principal halls to small private ones used by individual monks. Their basic pattern was a table or tables set out before a principal icon – which might be very large indeed – either sculpted in relief, or painted on the rear wall, perhaps flanked by others. On the tables would be set out arrangements of smaller images, along with the offering vessels used at stages of the ceremonies. The offerings set out were emblematic of the five senses, that is, of selfhood and everyday attachments which all Buddhists aim to dedicate and return to the ultimate principle of Dharmakāya for which a chörten is a stand-in. The offerings usually consist of a fine cloth scarf for touch, food such as barley-cakes (*torma*) for taste, incense for smell, bell or trumpet sound for hearing, and butter lamp for consciousness.

11   Icons set above an altar are dwelling-places for their spiritual presences. They are invoked by mantras to acknowledge and receive offerings and participate, so creating a kind of 'theatre' of spiritual principles on the altar table. Musical instruments would be laid out ready to be used at appropriate points in the ritual. Altar-layout and rite together are where human and transcendent meet and combine.

Some of the most famous public ritual performances of old Tibet follow the basic altar-layout; for example the seasonal 'expulsion of demons' dance

Whirling a prayer-wheel

which masked monks at some monasteries perform in a public courtyard before a huge and complex painted icon unrolled and hung several storeys high for the occasion. The dancers in the courtyard would thus correspond functionally with the smaller sculptures on an altar table.

Small personal altars follow similar patterns. Individual monks and monastic or social groups would choose one of the major figures as a cult focus for their spiritual lives: the Buddha Amitābhā, for example, or an independent figure from the depths of the Indian past such as Hevajra or the ferocious black Mahākāla, and perform their own daily ceremonials in front of them. But in addition they might undertake special sequences of offering and meditative ritual over specific periods of time, rearranging the layout on the altar as required.

Chanted recitation is the basis of all Tibetan ritual. As well as communally chanting texts and beneficent mantras, both monks and laity use prayer wheels: little cylinders on vertical spindles with small swinging weights which contain *Oṁ maṇe padme Hūṁ* and other mantras and invocations inscribed on paper scrolls. To swing these round amounts to recitation, and people carry them everywhere, whirling them continually. Monasteries and big houses often contained large prayer wheels, swung round and kept permanently revolving by everyone who passes. Mantras and invocations are also inscribed on cloth flags raised high into the air to send their 'messages on the wind' out into the region of infinite and invisible spiritual movement: a Buddhist version of the ancient and surviving shamanic Bön-po practice.

Meditative visualizations

Among the Tibetan orders of monks and nuns many simply live their lives according to disciplines in which meditation plays some part. But there are others who undertake with determination long, physically and spiritually energetic meditative procedures. To meditate, it is first necessary to develop the capacity for one-pointed concentration, to still the mind, then to achieve the sustained, unbroken attention to hold the point in focus for a long time. (This is exactly what the Western culture of constantly varying distractions particularly destroys.) Once the technique has been learned, one can build up quite complex structures and sequences in the imagination. The monastic life is designed expressly to make this possible. To carry it to the highest point individuals may shut themselves off in mountain retreats. Certain monasteries maintain a collection of cave-cells high among the peaks for this purpose, and keep them supplied with basic food. But some monks go far off into the remote mountains to live in continuous meditation, either depending on wild plants for food, or being brought occasional supplies by the inhabitants of the nearest village. A few of them 31 become yogis, *Naljŏrpas*, people committed to the 'short path' and aiming for Nirvana in their present lives. Usually they enrolled among the followers of a specific Naljŏrpa teacher, who would trace his line of descent by initiation from major figures in the historical past called Siddhas. Four of the most famous were the mythically potent Indians Naropa, Tilopa, Sarāha-pāda, and Marpa. Padmasambhava was another who figures large in Tibetan art. Naljŏrpas underwent extraordinarily severe disciplines and long initiations in which sexual rites often played a part. They then undertook months-long or even years-long meditative procedures. Texts record some of them, in which imaginative visualization was elaborated into enormous and complex sequences. Much Tibetan art is intended to provide a basis for such visualizations.

The meditation procedures are based on old Indian methods of *sādhanā* common to all Indian religions. This consists of the meditator calling on personified spiritual principles by name, invoking them by chanting their mantras and then visualizing their presence as intensely as possible so as to identify completely with them.

A great collection of Buddhist sādhanās in Sanskrit, called the *Sādhanāmālā* or 'Garland of Sādhanās', listing hundreds of Buddhist personified principles, was compiled in India by about AD 600. It was translated whole into Tibetan, and commented on many times by Tibetan writers. It gives each personification its own colour and posture, perhaps a number of heads and a set of arms and hands which all either make particular meaningful gestures (*mudras*) or hold symbolic implements. These images are, of course, totally 'unrealistic' in any sense of the word. Broadly speaking they represent Buddhism's metaphysical energy-concepts condensed into persons. To invoke them and identify with them in meditative ritual is to realize their meanings to the full.

A form of terrible Herūka carrying a Khaṭvaṇga – club with impaled heads – a flaying knife and skull-cup filled with blood

Here is an example from the *Sādhanāmālā*, giving the sādhanā of a female personification well known in Tibetan art:

> The worshipper should conceive himself as Vajravarāhī whose complexion is red like the pomegranate flower, who has two arms, one face, three eyes, dishevelled hair, and who is endowed with the six favourable symbols. Her essence is the five spiritual knowledges and her nature is the pleasure of *Sahaja* [supreme spiritual conjunction]. In her right hand she holds the vajra [handled] *gri-güg* [flaying-knife], in her left a skull-cup full of blood, with a trident impaling heads in the crook of that arm. She stands in the *Pratyāhlīda* [dance] posture and tramples on the fierce Kālarātri. She wears a garland of freshly severed heads and licks the blood that trickles from them.

Vajravarāhī usually has four companions, and she is the consort of a major Herūka (Hero) figure.

The Indo-Tibetan meditative rituals demand a truly extraordinary capacity for prolonged attention and intense, unbroken concentration. They consist of visualizing spreads, towers and sequences of such visionary presences, chanting their mantras all the time to energize them. The arrangements of figures are radiant metamorphoses that explode out of the Void, spreading out in supernatural space, say, vast panoramas of palaces and gardens complete with different classes of inhabitants; withdrawing these progressively and condensing them into a nuclear set of mantra script-syllables upon the disc of the moon; then diffusing from this a halo of further coloured mantra-letters which each individually converts into a group of humanoid figures, spreading out like lotus petals in limitless space. This whole panorama may then contract into a single figure of blinding blue radiance, which shoots down into the meditator's heart as an arrow-like ray.

The plans of such meditative procedures, fully imagined dramas far more elaborate than this brief example, were developed over the centuries and designed to have specific spiritual results. Altar-layouts articulated the

The graveyard spirit of the Khaṭvaṇga

imagery for some occasions, but collections of Tanka paintings, especially, support the realization of such visionary procedures, though being static, they can only hint at their full richness.

A monk or nun might hold one or two Tankas of their own representing favourite icons, or take several out from the library-store to hang on a personal altar, where they would first lift the veil that normally covers them to awaken the figures and invoke the principles to take possession. They would then perform their ceremonies and utter mantras to activate the figures emerging from the sky-Void, and representing those aspects of Buddhist realization on which the ritual is based. The bodies of figures may have the colours of the Elements (*Dhātus*): yellow, green, blue, red, white or black – clear and bright for benevolent beings, dark-tinged for threatening energies.

Depicted at the foot of some Tanka paintings is a rather gruesome little collection of physical emblems of the human faculties formally arranged in offering vessels: wrenched-out tongue and eyeballs for the realms of taste, speech and sight, lopped-off ears and nose for sound and smell, severed hands for touch, wrapped in the normal Tibetan honorific gift-scarf of silk. This offering symbolizes the meditator's abandonment of his or her entire everyday self to the beings depicted. It harks back to the ancient world-wide sacrificial customs, practised by the Bön-po, in which animals were slaughtered and cut up as offerings. But Buddhists offer up not the bodies of other beings, but their own. One surviving Buddhist ritual, strongly tinged with Bön-po magic, is called *Chöd*, and is a devastatingly vivid enactment of this self-sacrifice. The words of the ritual have been published in English, and the French traveller Alexandra David-Neel has reported how she came upon a young monk practising the rite in a desolate tract of mountains.

When a monk (it is usually a man) wishes to perform *Chöd* and take the 'short path' to Enlightenment he has first to take long instruction from a teacher. Then he goes off alone to a remote place high among the mountains, where for days on end he enacts a long liturgical psychodrama, in the course of which he visualizes and experiences to the full his body, self and mind being totally dismembered, smashed, crushed and shredded to wretched bloody pulp. He calls upon all the carrion-eaters and evil demons of the universe to feast on it, and experiences them doing so. He thus re-enacts ritually the total, compassionate self-sacrifice of the Buddha in the previous incarnation, when he fed his own body to the injured and hungry tigress nursing cubs. He senses to the full the agonies of his flesh, and the anguish of his human consciousness shattering. He returns effectively reborn. Such a voluntary descent into utmost obliteration has strong overtones of shamanic initiation.

Female Wisdoms and the subtle body

Female figures often appear in Tibetan art in sexual union with male counterparts. The females may be referred to as 'Wisdoms', since they personify particular kinds of intuitive insight, the wisdom of selflessness, while the males personify spiritual method or means. Strict Western interpreters often refuse to admit that the Wisdoms were derived from older Indian figures of Shakti which personify 'energy' or 'powers' imbuing the world, both in sexual union and on their own. But in the Tibetan context it is certainly not wrong to take Wisdom as the insight which potentiates method, for neither method nor wisdom alone can achieve any valid result. In addition, the sexual union carries the deliberate implication that the highest level of achievement is experienced as a transcendent bliss, for which the Sanskrit term *Sahaja* was used, and for which sexual delight was both a prime metaphor and a practical method.

22–3 The joined couple is called in Tibetan *yab-yum*, 'father-mother'. Of the four main schools of Tibetan Buddhism, the oldest, Nyingma, practises tantric rituals in actuality, whereas most initiates of the other three schools practise symbolically, through visualization. There can be no doubt, however, that sexual union was used in original Vajrayāna, both as a way of transmitting initiations through a line of female power-holders and as a basis for meditative ritual. We know that the great celibate poet-saint Milarepa was initiated partly through intercourse with a disciple of his teacher Marpa, and some of the most sacred texts of this branch of Buddhism, for example the *Hevajra Tantra*, give clear instructions for the way sexual ritual is to be performed. Its human practitioners become at the outset respectively Herūkas (Heroes) and Yoginīs (female Yogis) or Dākinīs, in Tibetan 'Khadomas' or female 'Sky-goers'. Both these terms are used for symbolic figures in Tibetan art, Dākinīs being female partner-figures whose names sometimes clearly identify them as forms of wisdom.

The sexual rituals both actual and imaginative on which the imagery is based depend upon a special technique that Vajrayāna developed for activating a subtle body within the meditator's physical body, with its own inner pattern of energies and channels. The principal channel runs between the perineum and space beyond the crown of the head. Through the crown, the energies of world-creation flow downward, to be converted and diffused through the mind and body so as to spread out the everyday world. The world-energy is latent most powerfully in the sexual energies. The meditator aims to gather these energies back into his or her system, reconcile, reconvert and condense them into a radiant spirit, called *Bodhicitta*, in which body, speech and mind combine. This Bodhicitta is driven progressively up along the central channel, absorbing three principal levels marked by lotus-like circles, towards the Void beyond its summit – to attain which is Nirvana.

The body is the agency which projects around each person his or her world, filled with all its stains and attachments to narrow and limiting things, objects of desire and hate that generate Karma, so the Buddhist uses every possible resource to gather and reconstitute the wasted outflows. First, however, it is necessary to energize the psycho-physical organs through which the projection-wastage occurs to their maximum, and then reverse the direction of flow. The most potent resource for doing this is sex.

The circles of the psychic body are identified with, and function through, the Skandas, the Elements, and the various kinds of emotion. First, the meditator has to identify each of these components in the field of his or her diffused world-experience; then precipitate them into humanoid figures. Each figure represents the spiritual condition in which the combined energies of one Skandha, one Element and one particular emotion are realized and then condensed. The meditation process consists in combining and concentrating each group at successively higher levels in the subtle body into the Bodhicitta, eventually reconverting the entire spectrum of

The chörten, symbol of unity and the levels through which it is attained in meditation. The levels also represent the five Elements: square base for earth, round dome for water, conical spire for fire, umbrella for air, seed-pinnacle for mind-essence

those energies simultaneously. For the male meditator, the concentrate is precipitated as a figure of a Dākinī, who (as Wisdom) personifies non-selfhood, *Nairātmyā*, far more to be desired then any outer partner. 'She' thus absorbs all the individual's desires which normally flow outward and focuses them inward. The male Herūka performs the corresponding function for the female meditator.

In the early stages of such Vajra-meditation, human partners meditate coupled together in sexual intercourse, taking care not to expend their contained energy outward, but reversing its flow in a process called *parāvritti*: turning back up. In later stages neither man nor woman needs an outer partner, for each has generated his or her own inner partner, gathered in and condensed from their own bodily world-projecting faculties. Union with these inner partners – the other halves of their true creative selves – produces a blissful experience (*Sahaja*) far more intense than any possible physical delight. Male and female have each become Herūka-Dākinī combined; eventually Buddha-Nairātmyā, which equals Enlightenment in union with Void. This is the subtle meaning of *Oṁ maṇi padme Hūṁ*. Even when no coupling is expressly referred to in the art or ritual, bi-unity is always implicit.

During these long yogic rituals, meditators evoke and visualize many orders of metaphysical principles, focusing them through mantras and humanoid images. The process of inward ascent through the levels of the subtle body is represented in art in different ways. Individual figures or pairs may represent its stages, each meant to be progressively expanded, assimilated and absorbed. Spirit guardians may be invoked to protect the participants.

The ultimate pattern

The mandala is one of the principal layouts used in all Tibetan mysticism and art. It consists of a circle with divisions radiating from the centre, sometimes interpreted as the petals of a lotus. This expresses the notion that the figures or features in the periphery are unfoldments from the centre; and once the mandala is visualized and vitalized, it may be infolded and returned to the centre. The mandala also integrates the relationships between principal figures at the central focus and others around the periphery. The mandalas of different lineages of deities may have varying numbers of 'petals'. Whole buildings may be laid out as mandalas; but most often we encounter them in paintings.

During meditation or ritual the mandala figures invoked are kept in states of radiant presence. A figure does not just disappear when it gives place to another. It may either be absorbed into the successor or continue to emanate from it. Many of the principal figures emanate extra versions of themselves, and the same figure may appear in different forms during different rites. Each mandala is meant to be set up and followed through, stage by stage, around its layout, beginning with its eastern or southern quadrant and ending at the centre.

There is one fundamental and widely used grouping of mandalas which correlates all the chief iconic figures of the Vajrayāna, identified by their colours, postures, gestures and the implements they hold. It was probably fully developed by the fifteenth century, and appears in slightly different versions (see p. 93).

26

20, 34

The ground: the Guardians of the Four Directions

The first mandala is focused at the centre of where the meditator sits on a covering of grass or a rug laid on his or her own ground (not on the earth), establishing the set of directions: East, West, North, South. (This orientation-pattern is continued through the three higher mandalas.) The meditator visualizes, facing out around the bodily seat into the four directions, a set of four ferocious guardian-kings, perhaps with fierce female counterparts, and then imagines the central channel of his or her own subtle body as the central axis of the entire universe. The guardians both 'protect' the meditator from being influenced by external phenomena in the directions, and control and concentrate his or her energies.

At the heart level: the five Peaceful Dhyāni Buddhas

The meditator gathers in his or her energies from the outside world through each of the directions in turn into the lowest inner realm of the body, in the belly. The watery element dissolves and combines them there with the central sexual energy to set them on the first stage of their ascent up the central subtle channel. At the fiery elemental level of the heart the energies enter the region of the chief iconic figures, five Peaceful Dhyāni Buddhas, four at the cardinal directions, who spread horizontally around the centre. Each Buddha (see p. 29) has a meaningful name and a 'family', and each inhabits a circular, halo-like realm of radiant light with a specific colour. The Buddhas may be envisioned in sexual union with their female Wisdoms. They are recognized as the Sambhogakāyas (visionary bodies) of five of the actual Buddhas (Nirmāṇakāyas) whom tradition records living successively during aeons of time before and after our own historical Buddha Gautama. They sit on a distinctive throne and wear a crown and jewels to indicate that they have attained all that the heart can desire, wealth and status beyond understanding. Each fuses into its 'domain' a Skandha, one of the human passions which normally distract people from realization, symbolized by a particular colour, an Element and a sense-region. Each Buddha sitting in meditation united with his Wisdom gathers together and unifies all the human urges, memories and Dharma-aspects belonging within his domain which the meditator is able to invoke, resolving them into a comprehensive experience of the Void.

The female Wisdoms are also sometimes called 'Tārās' and are ascribed different colours: Tārā means 'she who causes one to cross over the river of time and space to the uttermost shore'. Each Buddha family also comprises male and female Bodhisattvas who are projections of their central person.

The meditator realizes each Buddha region replete with all its family-factors, then concentrates it at the centre into a sixth Buddha figure, who symbolizes their combination. The combined energies coalesce as the 'seed of the five families', a joint energy identified with the Bodhicitta, the Vital Spirit, now personified by the female Nairātmyā. 'She' passes on, up the channel to the throat level, associated with Element air.

At the throat level: the Knowledge-holders

At the throat level the combination of the energies opens out to absorb a further mandala of middling-fierce 'Knowledge-holders' (see p. 94), each dancing in union with his female counterpart, together embodying a gnosis or deep combination of insights developed from the field of the corresponding Dhyāni Buddha. This mandala comprehends the region of speech, coherent utterance and image-formulation which guides the whole meditative process. The meditator energizes all the figures once more and combines them into a single figure, then passes the combination on up the radiant axial channel into the head-region of the Element mind, as a further transformation of divine Nairātmayā.

The head level, and beyond In the head region all is terrifying and 'unthinkable'. A final five-fold mandala spreads out composed of devastating and terrifying energies, Herūkas or Heroes haloed in flame (see p. 93) dancing in violent copulation with their no-less-terrific female complements. Very few meditators indeed are able to gain this region, or succeed in realizing and absorbing its stupendous energies. If they do, they may go on to reach a realm of the ultimate reality principle, towering over the summit of the subtle body, the habitation of a Supreme Principle, beyond Enlightenment, totally and blissfully united with the Supreme Wisdom. Different sects use different names for the Supreme Principle, which is the final revelation of the meaning of *Oṁ maṇi padme Hūṁ*.

Each family-line has been followed through at the successively higher levels of the subtle body in corresponding positions in the mandala. In a profound sense, each of the figure-types at different levels in each vertical 'family-line' is a modulation of a single metaphysical principle.

We already know that Buddhism's whole purpose is to abolish all spurious and confining entities, along with their negations and negations of negations, and to reach beyond them, so we take care not to treat these meditational figures and the concepts they embody as 'realities' of any kind, but understand them as helpful apparitions, explosions towards us from that Void out of which every illusory, limiting experience originates, to which meditation returns them.

The meditator in carrying through this process of visualization and transformation effectively participates in the stages of continuous creation in reverse, through the lowest to the highest levels of the cosmos. He or she also realizes the truth of the saying so often repeated in the texts of all the Buddhist schools: that Nirvana and Saṁsāra are 'not different', and experiences the inner meaning of the chörten as emblem of the Buddha-mind, the Darmakāya. The mutual dependence of Void and particular forms becomes as clear as day.

The structure embodied in the meditation-system of the psychic body provides the framework for the whole of Vajrayāṇa, and gives shape and significance to the life and activities of both monks and laity.

Death rites The ceremonial which Tibetan monks conduct for the dying reveals how deep-rooted this same system is in all phases of existence as well as in meditation. A text called the *Bardŏ Thödöl*, the *Tibetan Book of the Dead*, contains a long series of exhortations which the monks recite into the ears of a dying person over a period of many days, while he or she is supposed to be waiting in a kind of limbo – called the Bardö – before moving on to the next incarnation. As the person dies, as breathing, heartbeat and consciousness fail, the energies constituting the body continue to seek to aggregate afresh into another body. The traces of habit-energy which remain in the old body and have not been modified by Buddhist discipline and meditation govern what happens. The degree to which the dying person has controlled them determines the quality and status of the new aggregate. The monks performing the ceremony act earnestly and kindly, begging the dead person constantly to accept bravely the challenge of the brilliant coloured lights that appear on successive days, and reject the soft, seductive lights of the six realms of incarnation which appear alongside them. From time to time the monks utter a violent shriek – *Heeg* – intended to split the suture at the top of the cranium of the dead person to release the energies at favourable moments.

On those successive days the five Dhyāni Buddhas of the heart-level appear, as described, with their families, in an order corresponding, not with the meditative sequence, but with the realms of incarnation as they are given in the Wheel of Existences (p. 67). First appears the central Buddha, Vairocana, embodying the Skandha of mental formulation, in his intense blue light, accompanied by the alternative tempting soft white light which may lure the person of some achievement to incarnate in the realm of heavenly gods. Next appears Vajrasattva-Akshobhya in his intense white light, embodying the Skandha of form and accompanied by the alluring smoky light of the hells. Then appears Ratnasambhava in his strong yellow light embodying the Skandha of feeling, along with the soft blue light that calls the dying to reincarnate in the human world; then Amitābhā in his red light, embodying the Skandha of perception, appears accompanied by the soft yellow light that lures to the realm of hungry ghosts; then appears Amoghasiddhi in his green light, embodying the Skandha of constituting factors, accompanied by the soft red light that pulls the person to incarnate in the realm of struggling titans.

On the sixth day all five Buddhas appear in an overwhelming radiance. Then appear the Knowledge-holders accompanied by the lure to incarnation in the Sixth Realm of the animals. Finally, all forty-two deities of the Sambhogakāya appear, accompanied by a whole crowd of spirit-beings who attract the person towards all kinds of wombs. Eventually the dead person's energies aggregate, he or she enters a womb, and a new being is born at the karmic level it has earned.

Iconography of the system

Its iconography is the essence of Tibetan art. Every feature has clear and recognized meanings in relation to Buddhist doctrine and practise. The arrangements of the figures in the mandala diagrams evolved over centuries. The figures' meanings will only be properly recognized by someone who has experienced personally what they refer to. All are meant as stages that punctuate a continuum of spiritual progress.

There are three types of general symbols which identify the many different figures of mandalas and icons, and open up their deeper significance. Firstly, a figure may wear in its crown or tiara a small figure or head of another principal, indicating that it emanates from it. Ordinarily Buddhists think of their ancestral line of teachers as sitting in a stack above their heads. Then there are the gestures (*mudras*) that figures make with their hands, and thirdly, the implements that figures carry in their often multiple hands. The most frequently shown mudras are:

Earth-touching: the right hand points down to the ground, palm inward, finger-tips touching the earth, calling the earth herself to witness the

Buddha's self-dedication over the vast reaches of time and attainment of Enlightenment. The left hand remains on the lap.

Dispelling fear: the right hand is raised, palm out, fingers pointing up, offering protection, 'fear not'.

19 **Giving**: when the left hand is extended, palm out, fingers down, offering gifts and granting requests.

Preaching the doctrine: the two hands make an asymmetrical gesture with their fingers, 'turning the wheel' of the doctrine.

Deep-trance meditation: the hands are laid palms upward on one another in the lap, perhaps supporting a bowl or vase.

Blow-striking: one hand is raised to slap and so awaken to true reality.

Reverence and submission: hands joined palm to palm pointing up, fingers slightly bent.

Reverence for predecessors or teachers: forearm raised, fingers pointing to the same shoulder, palm down.

Menace: raised fist with extended forefinger.

Discussing: arm raised, palm out, fingers up, thumb and little finger bent across to meet.

Sprinkling: the hand has its fingers extended down into a vessel, to scatter the sacred blessings of the doctrine.

Revealing the subtle interplay of mutual causality: the hand is upright, palm out, only index and little fingers erect, the rest folded; symbolizes teaching the total interdependence of causes and conditions.

Revelation: forearm upright, hand held horizontal, palm up.

The implements and objects which figures may hold symbolize their actions, capacities and ritual processes:

Wheel: signifies the doctrine itself, especially referring to Karma.

37 **Vajra** (diamond): transcendent power of the doctrine.

Book: wisdom, which eliminates false assertions and negations.

Bell, usually with a vajra handle: primary vibration, the doctrine beyond ordinary hearing, emptiness.

Jewel, often framed in flame: supernatural and unimaginable originating radiance.

Lotus: unity unfolding into multiple manifestation, across the borders of common reality. Uncontaminated compassion.

Vase: container of the nectar of immortality gained by following the true doctrine.

Sword: the means of severing attachments, as shining wisdom cuts through limits and concepts.

Skull-cup, often full of blood: offering or surrendering of life-energy.

Severed head, singly or in a necklace of heads: the power of Time to deal death to the self-enclosed individual.

Double-skull drum: the dual nature of existence, conventional and ultimate reality.

Noose: the means to catch and strangle discursive thoughts.

Flaying knife, with an S-shaped blade, often with a vajra-hilt: the means of skinning away false selfhood and isolating boundaries.

Elephant-goad: the means of controlling powerful, elephant-like passions.

Bead rosary: power from recited mantras.

Skull-cup lined with silver, containing brain

Bow in right hand, arrow in left: the bow method, the arrow wisdom. Conventional and ultimate reality integrated.

Staff or club: slayer of conflicting emotions or delusions.

Club mounted with human heads: spiritual power to work magical effects.

Trident: the triple essence of time and its three horizons.

Fly whisk of yak-tail: implement for brushing away mental stains.

Snake, either held or as garland: vitalizing and creative but dangerous powers of the earth.

Anklet: the dance-music of Time.

Conch: the primal trumpet-sound calling all beings to the central truth.

Chain: the iron linkage of cause and effect of actions, Karma.

Scalp: skin from the top of the cranium and so infused with spiritual energy.

Knife: the cutter away of bonds.

Axe: cutter of the roots of illusion.

Enveloping flames: the fire of wisdom burning away ignorance.

Many heads: many identities compounded.

Ploughshare: breaker of hard-packed ground for the seed of Enlightenment to be sown.

All these attributes cross-connect the various figures and functions in the iconographic diagrams. The projective figures may be visualized as follows, according to the prescriptions in the *Sādhanamāla*:

Mandala of the four Guardians

The four Guardians are terrifyingly ferocious, big bellied, and dancing violently, face to face with female counterparts.

The Guardian of the South is usually YAMĀNTAKA, 'Conqueror of Death'. He is a powerful enchanter who has the head of a buffalo and a vast belly. His body is deep blue and he dances coupled with his blue consort the sow-headed PAŚUDHĀRĪ, 'Noose-holder', on a buffalo that may be copulating with a human. His hair stands up stiff and brown, he wears a tigerskin and has a garland of snakes. He holds a skull-cup full of blood and a white staff impaling a fresh-cut yellow head. He may also guard other directions, and he is connected obscurely with both the Bodhisattva Manjūśrī and the Buddha Akshobhya, who may be seen as the root manifestation of all Buddhas.

The Guardian of the West is the red-bodied, horse-headed HĀYAGRĪVA whose consort is the red, lion-headed VAJRAŚRĪNKHALĀ, 'Vajra chain-holder'. He carries vajra and staff, and has several heads, topmost the horse.

The Guardian of the North is white-bodied AMṚITADĀYA, 'Giver of Nectar', who carries a nectar-urn; his consort is the green, snake-headed KINKINADHĀRĪ, 'Bell-holder'.

The Guardian of the East is the green-bodied VIJĀYA, 'Conqueror', whose consort is white ANKUŚADHĀRĪ, 'Goad-holder', with a tiger's head.

[The Guardians may carry far more implements in far more hands than can be listed here. The meaning of the respective body-colours is given below, in connection with the Dhyāni Buddhas.]

After the first concentration of the meditator's energies, activated and collected by the Guardians, they may condense into the form of a red dancing female figure, the DĀKINĪ Kurukullā who first personifies Nairātmyā, the essence of abandonment of self, which becomes Bodhicitta.

Mandala of the Dhyāni Buddhas (heart-level)

This mandala is in the shape of a vast lotus with four main petals and a centre. Each sector contains a circular halo of radiance emanating from the Void, in which is seated one of the five Dhyāni Buddhas surrounded by members of his 'family', who represent his sub-functions.

In the South resides the Jewel family, in a yellow radiance from the yellow-bodied Buddha RATNASAMBHAVA, 'Jewel-born'. His throne is decorated with prancing horses. He holds the jewel in one hand and makes the gesture of giving with the other. He personifies the Skandha of feeling, the earth element; his sense-realm is touch; the human passion from which his energy is converted is pride, symbolized by the colour yellow. His female consort is MĀMAKĪ, who personifies the Wisdom of pride reversed. As Tārā she is yellow-bodied. The principal Bodhisattvas whom Ratnasambhava projects are the male Ākāśagarbha and the female Aparājitā. The Nirmāṇakāya (Buddha who lived in past ages) connected with him is Krakucchanda.

In the West resides the Lotus family, in a red radiance from the red-bodied Buddha AMITĀBHĀ, 'Boundless Light'. He sits in deep trance on a throne decorated with peacocks, holding a lotus. (He has an another form called Amitāyus, 'Limitless Life', who may be green and hold a vase of immortality-nectar.) He personifies the Skandha perception, his Element is fire, his sense-realm smell, the human passion his red colour symbolizes is desire or libido. His female consort is PĀṆDARAVĀRIṆĪ who personifies the Wisdom of passion transmuted, and as Tārā she is rosy pink. In his family he projects the most popular Bodhisattva AVALOKITEŚVARA, sometimes represented in Tibet as having 'a thousand' heads and arms. As patron of kings, Avalokiteśvara is sometimes called Lokeśvara, 'Lord of the Worlds', or Padmapāṇi, 'Lotus in hand'. Another male Bodhisattva he projects is Khasārpaṇa, and there are three female Bodhisattvas: KURUKULLĀ, Ekajatā and Dharmadhātvīśvarī, 'Lady Ruler of the Dharmadhātu. The Nirmāṇakāya connected with Amitābhā is our Buddha GAUTAMA.

In the North, the Sword family inhabits a green radiance from the green-bodied Buddha AMOGHASIDDHI, 'Productive Success'. He sits on a throne decorated with predatory Garuḍa-birds, and may hold a sword in one hand and make the gesture 'fear not' with the other. He personifies the Skandha 'constituting factors', his Element is water and his sense-field taste. The human passion from which his energy is converted is hate-filled envy, symbolized by the colour green. His female consort personifies the Wisdom of envy reversed, and as Tārā is green-bodied. The Bodhisattvas he projects are the males Viskambhin and Sarvaṇivaraṇa and the female Mahāśrītāriṇī, 'the great fruitful goddess of crossing over'. The Nirmāṇakāya connected with him is still in the far future: MAITREYA.

In the luminous blue-black region of the East resides the blue-bodied Buddha AKSHOBHYA, 'Unshakably Fixed', often regarded as the root of the other four Buddhas, so they may wear his figure on their crowns. He is the first in the order of creative descent, and head of the Vajra family. He sits on a throne decorated with elephants, holds a vajra in one hand and gestures 'touching the earth' with the other. He personifies the Skandha 'form', his Element is air, his sense-realm sound. The human passion from which his energy is converted is anger, symbolized by blue-black. His female consort is white LOCANĀ; as Tārā she is also white-bodied. The chief male Bodhisattva he projects is MANJUŚRĪ, the patron of the kings of Tibet, who also appears

36

27

35

in a terrifying form as VAJRABHAIRAVA (Terrible Vajra) with the most elaborate inconography of all Tibetan images. Vajrabhairava is usually in *yab-yum* posture, surrounded frequently with a great fan of thirty-six arms holding implements for the thirty-six branches of Enlightenment, and with sixteen legs for the sixteen types of avoidance, and the couple trample underfoot human and animal figures. He shows forwards seven of his nine heads, the uppermost that of Manjuśrī, the central that of a buffalo; he and his consort both have long red hair. Four of the female Bodhisattvas are Gangulī, Pratyangirā, another Tārā, and Mahācīnakramā. The Nirmānakāya with whom Akshobhya is connected is Kanakamuni.

In the blue region of the Centre sits the great fifth Buddha, the white-bodied VAIROCANA, 'Manifestor of Form', head of the Chakra or Wheel family, who sits on a lion- or dragon-decorated throne and holds a wheel. His Skandha is mental formulation, his sense-realm is sound, his Element mind, the subtlest of the Elements. The human passion from which his energy is converted is the dominant one of ignorant fascination, symbolized by the colour blue. His consort is the blue VAJRADHĀTVĪSVARĪ, Lady of a (yet higher) Vajra Element, and as Tārā she is white. His male Bodhisattvas are the great SAMANTABHADRA, 'All-good', who is the essence of all Bodhisattvas, as Vairocana is of all Buddhas, and often represented in art, and Kshitigarbha, 'Womb of the Earth', and females USNĪSAVIJAYĀ, 'Born from the Crown of the Head', and Sītapatrā.

19

Over the centre of all five Buddhas presides a sixth, VAJRASATTVA, who projects all the others. In meditative ascent, their energies combine and condense into him. He has no family. His radiance is an intense blue, his body is white, and he holds a vajra in each of his two hands. He is beyond Skandhas and sense-realms, but his Element is mind, the subtle matrix of all the other Elements. He sometimes has a white consort. He it is who embodies purest Bodhicitta, the 'seed of the five families', and rituals dedicated to him are always performed in secret. His projected Bodhisattva is GHANTAPĀNI, who holds a vajra in one hand and a bell in the other. He condenses the merit, compassion and skills of all the other Bodhisattvas. He has an extremely important and often-represented terrifying form, VAJRA-PĀNI, 'Vajra-in-hand', who is big bellied, blue-black of body, depicted with gold outlines, and always enveloped in flames. He has three huge eyes, and both holds and embodies the active power of the vajra, revealed in the entire Vajrayāna. His highest transformation of anger into wisdom is GUHYASAMĀJA, 'Secret Assembly', with his consort (p. 95).

Mandala of the Knowledge-holders (throat level)

The six Knowledge-holders dance standing face to face with their consorts. All are slender-bodied and only facially angry. Their colours are those of the five Dhyāni-Buddha families from which they are transformed, and their names define their natures.

To the South dances the yellow Jewel family's 'Power over Life's Duration', embodying the vision of everything as equal. To the West dances the red Lotus family's 'Lord of the Great [female] Symbol', who embodies the discerning wisdom of uttermost insight. To the North dances the green Sword family's 'Self-evolved Spontaneous Realization', half angry, half smiling. To the East dances the white Vajra family's 'Earth-abiding, whose mind is clarified and stainless like the Dharmadhātu'. The central Knowledge-holder, the fifth, is the red-brown, dominant 'Lotus Lord of the Dance' of the Chakra (Wheel) family, who embodies 'the total knowledge of all combined karmic consequences'. The sixth, above, is the blue-bodied CHAKRA SAṀVARA dancing with his red consort VAJRAVAHĀRĪ, 'Ḍākinī of all the Buddhas'. In him are condensed the essences of the other five.

9, 28

Mandala of the Herūkas (head level)

Here the huge, terrifying Herūkas dance standing in sexual union with their massive consorts, called 'Embracers'. All their faces are bloated with a violent rage which is the outer evidence of inner vajra-energy. All six arms are often winged. They, too, follow the same pattern-sequence as the Buddhas, and their colours are dark variants of those of the family-regions. To the South is RATNA-HERŪKA, who is tawny, has three faces, six arms holding (in pairs) jewel and bell, trident and scalp, staff and trident; his consort is Ratnakrotiṣaurimā. To the West is PADMA-HERŪKA, who is red-black, holding lotus and bell, trident and skull, club and drum; his consort is Padmakrotiṣaurimā. To the North is KARMA-HERŪKA who is dark green, holding sword and bell, trident and scalp, club and ploughshare; his consort is Karmakrotiṣaurimā. To the East is VAJRA-HERŪKA, who is dark blue-black, holding vajra and bell, two scalps, axe and ploughshare; his consort is Vajrakrotiṣaurimā. At the centre is BUDDHA-HERŪKA, who is brown, has three faces, and holds bell and wheel, scalp and sword, ploughshare and axe; his consort is the principal KROTIṢAURIMĀ, 'the Mighty Furious Mother'. The sixth, crowning, combination is VAJRAKĪLA, who is dull blue, a combined transformation of Vajrasattva and Chakra Saṁvara in union with VAJRAVARĀHĪ, whose sādhana has been described (p. 20).

9

The Adi-Buddha

Beyond all space and time, beyond all conceivable knowledge or performable act, sits the supreme pair, motionless and transcendent, often shown small to suggest their remoteness. The male is the Primordial (Adi) Buddha VAJRADHĀRA, in union with the white 'Mother of the Space of Heaven', or blue-bodied SAMANTABHADRA with his white consort. They wear no ornaments, make no gestures save meditation, carry no implements.

Different traditions sometimes recognize variant forms of Adi-Buddha, and the *Sādhanamāla* lists many subsidiary projections of the major figures who may be invoked for specific rituals.

We need to beware of treating these powerful figures in their systematic arrangement either as external or as merely conceptual, as something to observe, maybe to learn and think about. We should follow the psychological principle that 'the Gods are in us', and treat the Tibetan images as normally unrecognized aspects of our inner selves. Then when we study, assimilate and activate each one in turn, including its expressive actions, the meanings of its gestures and implements, its location in the system and sequence, we shall be discovering and re-integrating lost and fragmented parts of ourselves. Buddhism is doing, not thinking. To succeed at even the most modest level is a real step on the way towards Supreme Wisdom.

1 The power of Death is invisibly present in everything, everywhere. Against the black background of non-existence, he is recognizable here only through the shapes of his ornaments and attributes, which symbolize the energies by which we and all things seem to appear and disappear, without true beginning or end. Each meditator is intended to project his or her own image of Yama, the power of Death, within the shape of the enveloping ornaments. These energies include blazing fire, coiling snakes, the stripes on the flayed tiger-skin, the vortices of tempest; to the right a raging torrent and lightning-strike; to the left a tree of flame.

The invisible being holds a sword to cut away ignorance, a shamanic skull-club of spiritual force, the chain that binds wretched beings into cycles of Karma unhooked, and his own dragon of Time. Yama wears a garland of severed heads and the crown of the five skulls of the five Dhyāni Buddhas. Above hangs a decorative pelmet of flayed human skins from which dangle heads and eyes, feet and hands. The enraged buffalo-bull that Yama rides is somtimes shown coupling with the human figure he tramples. Two skull cups on either side are filled with white seed-energy and blood. The graveyard ground is scattered with dismembered bones. A tiny, terrified and adoring worshipper – with whom we as meditators identify – crouches at the lower left. (Meditation painting on cotton cloth, c. 18th century)

2, 3   The human skeleton plays a positive part in Tibet. It is not just an image of horror signifying the one and only end of everything. Buddhism teaches that all beings die many times over, to be reborn to new existences full of possibilities. Death is therefore a powerful and universal agent of transformation and spiritual progress, which only the foolish and wicked need fear. Buddhists become familiar with it, study it, contemplate its potentiality and learn to use it to move onward.

Human bone is the part of the body that survives longest after death, and many shamanic cults, including Tibetan Bön-po, treat bones whose owners have already passed to the realm of spirits as imbued with supernatural power flowing through them from that realm.

The pair of copulating skeletons painted on a wall of Dungkar monastery (left) symbolize Yama, the male energy of death that is present in all things, dancing embraced by the female Wisdom that knows and receives his nature as intimately as possible. The masked dancer in a seasonal ceremony (above) plays the role of Yama whose nature is ceaseless disappearance and change. (Chittapitri, mural painting in Dungkar monastery. Dancer at Kirintse monastery, Chumbi valley)

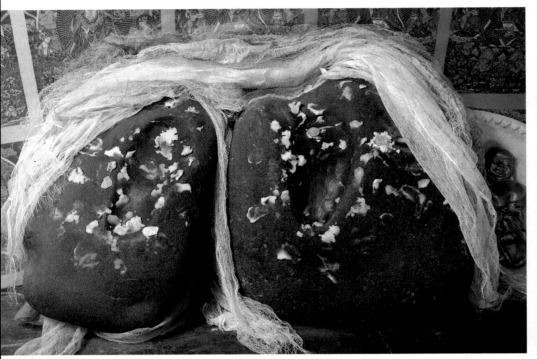

4, 5   Tibetans revere their tremendous landscape as sacred, filled with places and things which are centres of power or marked by great historical events. They express their reverence by adorning such holy spots and objects with offerings that include flowers, food and special white silk scarves, and inscribing them with mantras – syllables of power. In the monastery of Tetapuri, near the mountain Kailas, the most sacred in India and Tibet, the rock shown (above) is preserved and revered. It is marked with impressions said to be the footprints of one of Tibetan Buddhism's greatest founding saints, the Indian master Padmasambhava, as he alighted after flying from India. He was the central focus of the Nyingma or 'Old School' of Tibetan Buddhism, whose teachings and texts he brought with him from India. He had been initiated by a great female power-holding Dākinī before he attained Buddhahood. Elaborate and fantastic legends gathered around his name, and he is said to have performed many miracles.

The hillside in the foreground (right) confronts Mount Ahri that towers over the frozen lake Rawu. It is planted with a small forest of prayer-flags inscribed with mantras that fly in the perpetual wind to connect with the moving spirits of the air and disperse the mantra's benevolent power

6, 7, 8   In some monasteries the monks
perform dances which preserve
elements of the nature-spirit religion of
pre-Buddhist times, called Bön-po. The
monks take on the spirits embodied in
the masks by reciting incantations and
performing rituals. The dances are
usually seasonal; and by enacting the
ultimate triumph of benevolent forces
over evil, ensure that this will be the
outcome. Some of the spirits are local,
the benevolent ones Buddhist. Dancing
is the universal shamanic way of linking
up with the spirit world. The costumes
with their embroidered patterns, like
music, do the same. The small
sculptured figures (top right) are the
buffalo-headed Yamāntaka, 'Conqueror
of Death', dancing with his female
counterpart to display their spiritual
nature, the union of compassion and
wisdom, as do so many Tibetan figures.
(Photographs, 1911 and contemporary.
Yamāntaka, gilt bronze, 17th century)

9, 10, 11   The powerful image of Mahākāla, the 'Great Power of Time' (left), is a guise under which the Ultimate Principle shows itself, pointing to the absolute impermanence and unreality of the conventional world of separate things. He sits enveloped in fiery energy, waving a sword with a vajra-hilt and drinking from a skull cup of steaming blood. He wears as earrings two severed heads; and his crown of five skulls refers to the subtle doctrine that the five Dhyāni Buddhas, central images of Tibetan Buddhism, cannot, in common terms exist. At the centre below dances great Buddha-Herūka, central figure of the topmost meditative mandala. Around the lower part skitter the animal-headed demons of old shamanism who act as his agents of death, change and return. A heap of skulls contains offerings. Level with Mahākāla are four of Tibet's guardian spirits, including the female Palden Lhamo, special guardian of the Dalai Lamas. Around the upper edge are ranged teachers and great successful beings from the past. And at the top centre sits the meditation-deity Chakra Saṁvara, embraced by his female consort Vajrahāri, essence of Wisdom. The vertical axis linking the three central figures shows that they are transformations of each other.

Above is a three-dimensional image of the same persona receiving offerings, and above left a monastic dancer masked as Mahākāla. (Tanka, painting on cotton cloth, c. 17th century. Altar figure, Drapung monastery, dancer, Hemis monastery)

12, 13   *Tibetans experience the power of the wind directly and harness its energy as sound in a variety of ways. Trumpets are one. The smaller here have a strident sound. The huge copper and brass conical ones give a deep, shuddering roar audible for miles. Trumpets are used to call on and warn the spirits of ceremonials. Monastic chanting is done in a deep vocal register to reach the spiritual foundations of the world. The crested hats are also ceremonial, their thousand strands symbolic of the thousand Buddhas of this era*

14, 15, 16 Monasteries are the strongholds of Tibetan Buddhism, distributing spiritual power through their functions as university, religious, artistic and administrative centres. The painting on the left illustrates aspects of life in monasteries of the Sakyapa tradition. In the right foreground an abbot in a tented enclosure is instructing monks. Another official is dealing with lay people. In the left foreground officials receive visitors wearing eighteenth-century Mughal and hill-Rajput dress. In the central enclosure sits an abbot receiving Indian and Chinese deputations. To the right artist-monks are painting on stretched cotton cloth. At the top left a text-study and discussion session is in progress; and at top right an abbot is preaching to monks and lay people. In the sky remote celestial beings preside. The actual monastery of the Potala at Lhasa, above right, is the spiritual and political centre of Tibet; right is the Yambulhakhang monastery in the Yarlung valley, Central Tibet. (Painting on cotton cloth, 18th century. Photographs, contemporary)

17, 18, 19   Phur-bus are spirit-daggers that embody the compelling power of the mantra Hūṁ. Gesturing with one of these phur-bus at the conclusion of a prayer or invocation a monk has uttered drives the invoked energy on its way. Every monk therefore needs a phur-bu to perform ceremonials and enforce their effects. Above, the phur-bus, each one different, will be used in four pairs, one for each cardinal direction and each half-direction, as the monks take up their positions forming the outer 'Guardians' circuit of a mandala during the ceremony of consecration of a place.

Above right, the boy-monk is a present-day Tulku, the latest reincarnation of an important dead lama in a line of Bodhisattva incarnations. He is making the elaborate gesture of 'the mandala offering of the universe', not only to display it, but to induce in himself, by making it, the inner states to which it refers. The figure (far right) represents the female Bodhisattva of Benevolent Wisdom 'Born from the Crown of the Head'. She is of the family of the great central Dhyāni Buddha, Vairocana. Her right hands are making, from the top, the gestures of 'revelation', 'displaying the subtle interplay of mutual causality', and 'giving' or 'granting': all aspects of her inner nature.
(Photographs, contemporary. Bodhisattva Uṣṇīṣavijayā, bronze, 18th century)

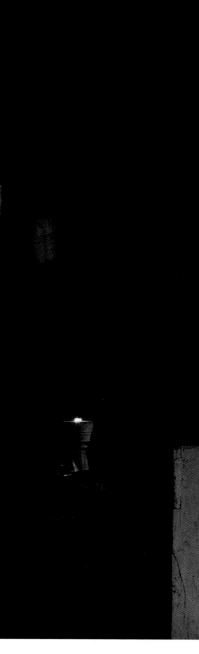

20, 21   *Preparing for an initiation ceremony, monks in Leh in Western Tibet (above) are colouring a mandala already drawn out on a piece of board by tapping out grains of coloured sand from little spouted containers. Some of the central power-emblems are already completed. When the ceremony is over the mandala will be obliterated, to be remade for the next ceremony.*

At the refugee monastery of Samye-ling in India (above right), the monks are performing a prayer service on behalf of all living beings. Two of the huge metal trumpets stand telescoped at lower right. Red pillars, bright coloured and embroidered hangings transform and spiritualize the hall, establishing it outside ordinary time and space

22, 23, 24 *Buddhism exists only as tradition, carried over the centuries by individuals within the order of monks and nuns who are thought to have accumulated great stores of merit, to which they themselves must never become attached. Right and below are two Mahāsiddhas – 'great achievers' – from the remote, semi-mythical era of Indian Vajrayāṇa. The painted figures,* right, *represent the Mahāsiddha Vajraghaṅta coupling in flight with his female partner; the bronze couple,* below, *perhaps Gaṅdhapa with his. Both couples illustrate the ancient practice of male and female meditators uniting as Herūkas (Heroes) and Dākinīs or 'Sky-goers' to complement and help concentrate each others' inner energies. Gaṅdhapa wears the five-skull crown of Mahākāla and holds the vajra and bell of the supreme Bodhisattva Ghaṇṭapāni which indicate his achievement of the Ultimate*

The couple at the right *represent the transcendentalized image of the Mahāsiddha pair, and at the same time personify the great mantra Oṁ maṇi padme Hūṁ. The male is holding a vajra emblem over the centre of a lotus. 'Maṇi', meaning 'jewel', is equivalent to vajra, 'diamond'. Padme means 'in the lotus', which refers to the receptive, creative and expansive energies. Vajra and padma also have the metaphorical significance of male and female genitals, so here 'vajra' is in 'padme' in the fullest sense, as the couple dance.*
(Vajraghaṅta, painting on cloth, 18th century. Gaṅdhapa, gilt bronze, 17th century. Mural painting, Gyantse, 15th century)

25, 26   The red Kurukullā, a Dākinī haloed in flames, represents the inner female energy of wisdom complementary to the male meditator's own. He may gather and focus that female energy, at first with the help of an actual female sexual partner who is an initiated 'power-holder'. The bow and flowery arrow signify the union of method and wisdom, the power of love. In common life energy is dispersed into creating each individual's body, life and world. Condensed and glowing red as that energy concentrated, the Dākinī transcends and tramples down the ego symbolized by the ordinary body. In her crown she wears the skulls of the five Dhyāni Buddhas. As she ascends through the subtle body she projects and then withdraws the mandalas at each level, herself metamorphosing at each stage to become total non-selfhood. Left, she is carved, seated, on the bone plaque at the crossing of a monk's ceremonial ornament. Right, a Tanka painting shows her iconography. (Photograph, contemporary. Tanka, 18th century)

27, 28   The visualizations used in
meditation form an ascending sequence.
All are manifestations of Vajra, Supreme
Power. The Dhyāni Buddha Akshobhya
at the heart level, head of the Eastern,
Vajra family (above), is visualized in
union with his white Wisdom,
surrounded by four Bodhisattvas who
express his compassion. He is usually
taken as the 'first' of the four directional
Buddhas, and appears in a rainbow halo.

The upper central figure in the Tanka
(opposite) represents the transformation
of Akshobhya into Vajrasattva, the
Buddha who encapsulates the energy
and wisdom of all five Dhyāni Buddhas.
Around him are shown the historical
Buddha Gautama and three
Bodhisattvas. The chief central image is
blue-bodied Chakra Saṁvara, the Great
Bliss who is the crowning sixth and
condensed essence of all the

Knowledge-holders (pages 31, 92). He
dances coupled with his red Wisdom,
essence of all Dākinīs. His multitude of
hands, implements and ornaments
show the vast range of his insights and
powers. Below are Mahākāla at the right,
and a version of the Guardian of the
East. (Akshobhya, detail of mandala
shown complete on p. 93. Kālachakra
Tanka, painting on cotton cloth, 19th
century)

29, 30   A rock near Lhasa is painted to invoke the presence of three great spirit beings. Below is the tantric deity Yamāntaka, destroyer of enemies, whose protective presence is also invoked at the outset of meditation. Above are the founders of two of the main traditions of Tibetan Buddhism: Tsongkapa in his pointed yellow hat, founder of the Gelugpa tradition, and Padmasambhava, founder of the Nyingma tradition, in his ear-flapped red hat. Attaching scraps of cloth is an almost universal human symbolic custom for affirming faith and praying for protection.

Devotees making a pilgrimage to the sacred mountain Kailas repeatedly measure out their own length over the entire journey. They wear 'shoes' on their hands to protect them from the harsh rocks. This mode of pilgrimage, by exaggerating the difficulty of the journey, expresses the maximum devotion. It has long been the fulfillment of a standard vow

31, 32   *The Nyingmapa monk*
meditating (above) *is probably on the*
'one-life short-path'. The ferocious
power that he must confront is
represented (right) *wearing an ascetic's*
hairstyle and crossed body-belt.
(Mahākāla figure, silver studded with
turquoise, c. 16th century)

33, 34 *Stupa-chörtens large and small are emblems representing total Enlightenment, Parinirvana. Above, the central object is an ancient stone stupa carved probably in the ninth century at Bodhgaya in India, the sacred site of the Buddha's Nirvana. Its four faces bear small Buddha figures, and its structure symbolizes the totally Enlightened being.*

Here it is the focus of a ceremony at Leh at which thousands of Tibetans circumambulated the stupa, lighting candles to demonstrate and perpetuate its radiance, offering prayers for the now-exiled Dalai Lama.

On the right *the painted mandala represents the chörten in plan view. Its central summit carries the mantra Oṁ maṇi padme Hūṁ, and its sixteen surrounding terraces represent sixteen levels of attainment on the way to the Buddhist goal. Above are patron figures; below is Tārā, incarnation of Wisdom, and Mahākāla once more. (Kālachakra, 'Wheel of Time' ceremony, Mahabouda stupa, contemporary photograph. Kadampa mandala, c. 1900)*

35, 36, 37 *These three small altar figures summarize the aims of the entire Buddhist faith. The upper figure on the left represents the compassionate Bodhisattva Manjūśrī, who personifies the whole wisdom of Buddhist teaching. He is seated on a lion, whose resonant roar the voice of the doctrine resembles. He makes the gesture of 'preaching', and from him spring shoots and lotus blossoms. On his left shoulder-lotus is balanced a book of Wisdom.*

The lower figure on the left is that form of the compassionate Bodhisattva Avalokiteśvara which embodies the universal mantra Oṁ maṇi padme Hūṁ, chanted continually by all Tibetans. He holds the recitation rosary and the lotus.

On the right is the Bodhisattva-form of Vajrasattva in whom are condensed the essence of all Buddhas, Bodhisattvas and Wisdoms, symbolized by the four-pointed vajra he holds. The bell represents both the doctrine beyond hearing, and emptiness, the vajra the compassionate means to benefit others.

Images like these are always hollow, and the opening beneath was usually closed by a metal plate after the interior had been filled with paper strips inscribed with prayers and pieces of fine coloured cloth, intended both to honour and invoke the presence of the image's power. (Manjrūśrī, gilt bronze, 18th century; Avalokiteśvara, brass with semi-precious stones, early 16th century. Ghantapāṇi, gilt bronze, c. 18th century)

38   *The painting (left) represents the second Panchen Lama (1485–1505) holding a book, with the first Panchen Lama in a rainbow on the upper left. Between them is the teacher Tsongkapa who links them. The Panchen line, centered on the Tashilhunpo monastery shown at the left, is supposed to be the purely spiritual, as against political, head of the Buddhist community in Tibet. He sits under a peach tree that symbolizes Paradise. At the top right is the Supreme Bodhisattva Chakra Saṁvara, inhabiting the tree and wearing the stripped-off skin of the elephant of ignorance, coupled with his red Wisdom-Dākinī of the knowledge of the emptiness of all self-identity. In the centre below a monk reads a sacred book, as transmitter of the doctrine. At the bottom left appears Palden Lhamo, spiritual guardian of the Dalai Lamas; at right is the red Guardian of the West, Hāyagrīva. (Tanka, painting on silk, 18th century)*

Right, silver hand holding a vajra, symbolizing the essential power of Tibetan Buddhism

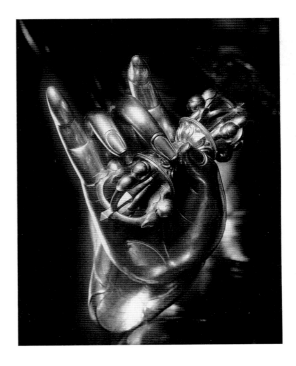

The Buddha

Our Buddha Guatama preached his first sermon, the basis of all Buddhist teaching, in the Deer Park at the city of Sarnāth, and spent the rest of his life teaching and building up his order of monks, of which the Tibetan is one branch. The Indian sculpture from Sarnāth of the Buddha preaching his first sermon, *left*, shows the pattern followed by all later images, like the Tibetan painting, *below left*, illustrating the events of his life.

At his Enlightenment the Buddha saw into all his thousands of previous lives, during each of which he had performed acts of total self-sacrifice, so gaining the vast store of merit, Karma, that brought him to Nirvana. Stories about those lives provided Buddhism's models of conduct.

The First Sermon contains four Holy Truths. First: all existence entails suffering. Second: suffering results from cravings and greed that whirl one through incarnation after incarnation. Third: one abolishes suffering by extinguishing cravings and greed. Fourth: the route to such extinguishing is the Buddha's Holy Eightfold Path, described in all Buddhist teaching.

The Wheel of Existences, *opposite*, summarizes the doctrine, illustrating the cycles in the grip of the red monster of Time. Its six sectors represent the six realms of rebirth referred to in the *Book of the Dead*, or *Bardö Thödöl*; clockwise from the top: gods (whose lives though long and superficially happy still end in suffering), titans, hungry ghosts, hells, animals and finally humans. In each, a humane Buddha-form offers salvation. At the hub are images of the urges that keep the cycles whirling: cockerel for greed and desire; pig for delusion and ignorance; snake for hatred and aversion. Around the rim are images of the twelve experiences, including Skandhas, fragmentary experiences that shape delusory existences. Clockwise from the top: blindwoman for ignorance; potter for Karmic formations; monkey for agitated consciousness; houses with six windows for the six senses; two men in a boat for name and form; pair of lovers for close contact; arrow in eye for feeling; drinker served for thirsts; gathering fruit for clinging; sexual intercourse for becoming; giving birth for birth; carrying a corpse for the burden of death. Above, the Buddha points out the eight-spoked wheel of his Path. (Stone sculpture, Indian, c. AD 420. Tanka, 18th c. Detail of Wheel of Existences, 20th c. Wheel, Tanka, 20th c)

Death and bones

The sites where dead bodies are disposed of are numinous places to every culture. Tibetans use several methods of disposal, but since wood is scarce they do not usually cremate. Mostly they expose the cut-up remains on a high open place to be consumed by scavenger-hordes of beasts, vultures and crows *(top right)*, whose roles are reflected in the demon masks of the dance-drama. Human bones are used for all kinds of implements. Cups and drums are made from skulls, trumpets from thigh-bones, aprons and necklaces from smaller pieces *(left and bottom right)*. Human skin is used for drum-heads and parts of costume.

The funeral-ground belongs to Yama, Lord of Death. To the Buddhist, time and death are not simply agents of final destruction, but represent the transformation which the ending of one life brings as prelude to opportunities in the next. So the Buddhist needs to face out and accept fully the natural fear and horror which everyone feels at the presence of death, and realize the illusory nature of 'end' as well as 'beginning' of self and things. To do this, the dedicated devotee may live and meditate in a funeral-ground; or perhaps perform the Chöd rite of total self-destruction described on page 21. The ritual flaying knife, *centre right*, is a symbol of the stripping away of the false skin of selfhood. (Dākinī with bone ornaments, Nepal, 18th c. Human bone ornament, Gyantse. Skeletons or *Chitapittri*, painting, *c.* 19th c. *Gri-güg* or ritual flaying knife, 18th c. Human bone apron 19th c)

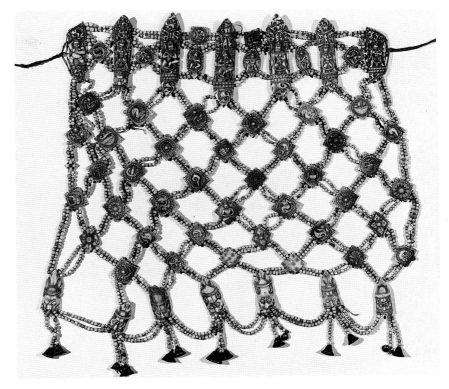

After his death and attainment of complete or Parinirvana the Buddha's body was cremated, and fragments of his charred bones, teeth, hair and robe were distributed around the Buddhist world as holy relics. They were at first placed in the tops of tall mounds, which gradually evolved into built structures called stupas, the prototypes of all dagobas, pagodas and Tibetan chörtens. Even without relics, chörtens became pure symbols for the ultimate attainment (which must actually be realized as *no*-attainment), Parinirvana. Their levels from ground to peak came to stand for stages on the way, the whole standing for the invisible and universal Dharmakāya in two principal modes. First, the shaped levels are equated with the five Elements, square base with earth, round dome with water, conical spire with fire, umbrella with air, peak-finial, shaped as a flaming seed-drop, with mind-essence. Second, each whole is taken as structurally analogous to the inner unity reconstituted in the individual by meditation.

All Tibetan monasteries centre on chörtens, which are built first, as shown in the painting of the construction of the first monastery in Tibet, Samye-ling *(far left)*. It is considered highly meritorious to build, model or paint as many chörtens as possible. Individuals might own small ones like that shown *centre*, as a focus for meditation.

At the Potala, the capital monastery of Tibet *(above left)*, the chörten stood on flat ground below, at the entrance to Lhasa, because one of the main rituals of reverence performed by monks and laity consists of walking around a chörten sunwise, keeping it on the right hand.

Above, a monk pours out water for offering bowls in front of a modern altar on which stands a chörten wrapped in the standard honorific white silk scarf, among other icons. The village shrine at *left* is given the significance of a chörten by the umbrella crown. (The Potala, with chörten now destroyed, photograph 1904. Samye-ling monastery, detail of Tanka, 18th c. Bronze chörten, 12th c. Altar, contemporary photograph. Shrine building, Tarap, Dolpo)

Dance-drama

Religious dance rehearses the act of creation, returning the participants back to an epoch 'before' the degraded present, reinstating the 'original' *status quo* and restoring the realm of spirits. In many Tibetan monasteries various kinds of masked dance-dramas used to be performed by monks to huge audiences of lay-people and monks who travelled in from far and wide. Most were based on vanished Indian prototypes. Some recounted stories of the Buddha's lives, others crucial and beneficial events of Tibetan history which had attained mythical status, such as the story of Padmasambhava who established Buddhism in Tibet in the eighth century. Some are seasonal ceremonies, such as the 'scapegoat' dances in which evil, represented by the dancers, is cast out. There is always a large number of performers wearing masks made of papier-maché, wood or thin copper sheet which transform them into the spirit beings represented by their masks (*far right*). Performances last many days.

The whole dance-drama is carried on to varied music. It begins with a stately procession of monks, perhaps dressed in the black robes of pre-Buddhist times. After this appear troupes of demonic maskers, leaping, shrieking, whistling and banging drums to fast and agitated music, and wearing the heads of oxen, snakes, tigers, vultures and dragons, or skull-masks and skeleton costumes. Similar demonic figures appear in paintings. Further solemn masked processions of chanting Buddhist saints, often headed by Padmasambhava (above), drive the demons away, and perform a stately rotary dance. Clowns provide light relief. Earlier a figure made of dough has been prepared, complete with its coloured inner organs, perhaps including pieces of actual human flesh.

This is ceremoniously loaded with all the evils of the world, and violently stabbed and torn by returning demons. Yamāntāka 'destroyer of death', wrathful deities and monsters continue the dance, which concludes with a ritual triumph of benign Buddhist figures. ('Scapegoat' dance, Jo-khang, Lhasa. Monks practising dances, viewed from the roof of Hemis monastery, Ladakh, and the arrival of the masked Padmasambhava, contemporary photographs. Three masked dancers, Tigpa monastery, contemporary photographs)

Books and wisdom

Books and monastic libraries are revered as physical embodiments of faith, doctrine, and especially wisdom – who is portrayed as a golden female figure in the Tanka painting shown *far right*. Tibetans as they read mentally rehearse the shape and sound of each letter, as contributing to the whole meaning of the text. Originally the Buddha and his early followers taught by preaching out loud to their audiences, most of whom were illiterate, so the earliest teachings were all memorized. Preaching still remains a most important activity for monks. But as monasteries grew up in India, and libraries developed, monks were able to write and so preserve and transmit all sorts of intellectual disciplines, and experienced monks taught their students by explaining and commenting on written texts. Monasteries became intellectual

powerhouses, their monks skilful administrators, engineers and mathematicians as well as mystics. Buddhist philosophy, as yet little studied in the West, reaches far beyond the problems with which we are normally familiar.

In north-eastern India, from where Tibet received Buddhism, great vanished monastery-universities contained huge libraries of manuscripts dealing with all kinds of subject matter, copies of which were carried to Tibet, There they were re-copied, translated, and later printed from woodblocks, in a beautiful script *(right)* derived from Indian Nāgarī, which is held sacred.

In India books were usually written horizontally on strips from between the veins of palm leaf, held stacked in order by being strung on cords. Traditional Tibetan books follow this

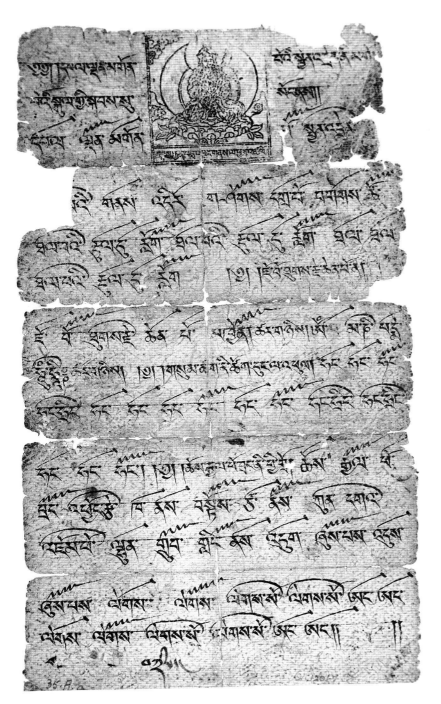

format – though without the cords –
but since the Chinese invasion more
are printed in the upright format. Their
pages are large, and are kept wrapped
up in cloth closed between heavy
boards, often finely carved with
decoration (centre left) that testifies to
their sanctity. They are stored on
shelves (top left).

Wisdom is a key term in Buddhism,
derived from an ancient corpus of
Wisdom literature, centred on one of
the oldest Buddhist mantras: Oṁ gate
gate paragate parasaṁgate bodhih
svāhā: 'Oṁ [the mantra of nuclear
reality] – gone gone, completely gone,
totally crossed over [beyond the
furthest shore]. Enlightenment. Svāhā
[syllables with the sense, 'let it be so']'.
Tibetan Buddhism is full of varied
female personifications of Wisdom
'gone beyond the furthest shore',
including the Tārās, whose name
comes from the word that means
'causing to cross over'. (Books in the
library, and monks reading, Gyantse.
Wooden binding-board, 15th c. Tanjur
book-cover with page in Mongolian
script, 18th c. Tanka of Goddess of
Supreme Wisdom, 18th c. Prayer sheet
with recitation notations, 19th c)

The realm of sound

Tibetan Buddhism condenses all the modes of human experience into its ceremonials and meditative imagery. The visual arts embrace the visual realm, music and sonic implements the sound realm. The medium of sound is the air, which we know most intimately as our personal breath by which we live and utter, and through which we intuit frequencies of vibration. Chanting, trumpet and flute-like playing, drumming and bells all focus sound; and the shapes of musical performance focus varied patterns of sound. The aim is to experience the Whole via sonic unity, identified in Kashmiri doctrines transmitted to Tibet as *Nādabindu*, sound-seed, or *Spandu*, primal vibration. A figurative embodiment of the air, *below*, is the Garuḍa-bird, a spirit-being known in all Indianized cultures.

Ornate trumpets are formed from conch shells, *right*, commonly used in ceremonies the world over, and ancient Indian emblems for the Primal Sound. Their deep resonant roar is matched by Tibetan vocal chanting and the sound of massive metal trumpets. The double-skull drum, *bottom left*, another old Indian emblem of cosmic vibration, is played by a rotary flipping movement that makes its tethered bead strike alternately each of the skins. Its two sides symbolize the dual nature of reality: the conventional reality and the ultimate. The bell with a vajra handle, *centre left*, yet another symbol of the Primal Sound, can also

be used as a sonic focus for meditation by rubbing its rim gently and continuously with a stick, so producing a sustained, small ringing hum.

Musicians enlist the powers of ritual music in ceremonial like that *right*, performed for a dead person. The monk reading a book with his instruments hung around him *(below right)* is uttering and experiencing inward sound. (Thigh-bone trumpet, bell and drum, implements used during the 'cutting the ego' ritual, contemporary photograph. Meditation bell and stick, *c.* 1800. Double skull drum, 19th c. Garuḍa-bird, woodcarving, 18th c. Musicians, contemporary photograph. Conch trumpet, 18th/19th century. Lama reading, Tarap, Dolpo)

Tibetans use mantras in many ways. A mantra consists of one or more syllables which are held to condense and precipitate energies, either for ritual or magical purposes. *Oṁ maṇi padme Hūṃ* is the best known (see p. 16), but there are many others, each with a different effect. *Oṁ* features in many of them. It originated in India several centuries BC, where it is considered the seed-sound. Reciting it properly, each individual experiences in it the world's countless voices, cries, songs, all noises of nature and the

wind, and even the inner frequencies of cosmic structure. As well as *Hūṃ*, another mantra-syllable that directs energy is *Phaṭ*. Mantras only work if learned and uttered 'properly', with total concentration of that mind from which all forces originate. Uttering them so can even affect one's Karma.

Mantras are essentially sonic, but they can also be precipitated visually as the sacred Sanskrit letters which have been their vehicles from time immemorial – even by people who do not know Sanskrit, provided they

execute them properly. Most single-syllable mantras are based on the first syllable of a word or name, ending with one of the great powerful letters: especially the long-drawn nasal humming (ṁ), or sharp *k* or *ṭ*. Ordinary words, however sacred like *maṇi padme*, 'jewel', 'lotus', are given their force by the power-syllables which frame them.

Many Tibetans recite their great basic mantra *Oṁ maṇi padme Hūṁ* almost continuously. This is supposed to help consolidate its beneficial effect.

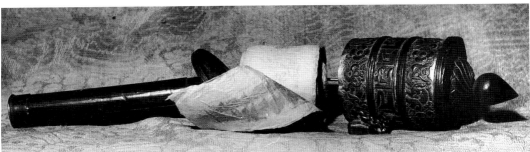

They enlist the wind to help repeat it by inscribing it on flags (*far left*). They turn endlessly prayer wheels of all sizes, hand-held like those at *top* and *above*, or set up in halls like that at *right*. They incise it on rocks by roadsides, *top left*, or paint it round the circumference of a circle, *left*, or write it on paper slips they wear in charm boxes hung round their necks. (Stone incised with *Oṁ maṇi padme Hūṁ*. Prayer flags and mani stones, Tso Mapam, Lake Manasarova, contemporary photograph, Mantra mandala painting, 19th c. Pilgrims with prayer wheels and rosaries, contemporary photograph. Prayer wheel and paper roll, 18th c. Great prayer wheel, Samye Lhakhans monastery, Yarlung valley, contemporary photograph)

Phur-bu and vajra

Tibetan Buddhists took over from the old shaman-magicians of both India and Tibet the custom of using their own power-charged implements in their rituals. All newly-made implements have to be initially charged-up with power by rituals and mantras performed by specially qualified monks, but old implements, which have belonged to distinguished magicians or saints and been used by them, have an extra potency.

The phur-bu, literally 'nail' or 'spike', is sometimes called a 'magic dagger' because it has a long triangular blade and a hilt worked with the face of its indwelling spirit or a vajra, or both. It is the physical embodiment of the power of the mantra *Hūṁ* (inscribed at the centre of the crossed vajras, *centre right*). Monks performing rituals gesture with it, either singly or in groups, to enforce the effect of mantras and complete ceremonies. They stab it towards the direction or directions in which they mean the recitations to take effect.

The vajra (*below* and *facing page*) embodies the power of the entire Vajrāyaṇa doctrine and practice. The shape is usually double-ended, each end consisting of a central prong enclosed by two or more incurved prongs; others may have four or eight ends. Vajras are added to all kinds of ritual implements to potentiate them — bell and hammer, *left*, skull-cup offering vessel, *below right*.

The vajra or *Dorje* encapsulates the meanings: 'lightning strike' as maximum active energy; 'diamond' as the densest and sharpest of gemstones; 'male penis' as the source of the creative seed, which is identified with the Bodhicitta, essence of Enlightenment (*Thig-le* in Tibetan). The 'jewel in the lotus' is vajra in the feminine unfolding universe.

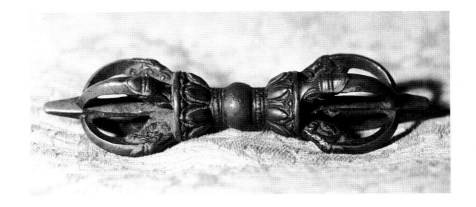

A small vajra set on a lotus-pedestal – maṇi padme – like that *above left* may be used for meditation. *Below*, a vajra-handled bell and vajra in ceremonial use in a nomad's tent.

(The Dalai Lama hammering a phur-bu during a ceremony of consecration of a sand mandala, contemporary photograph. The deity of the phur-bu, detail of scroll painting. Painted wood phur-bu, 19th c. Bronze phur-bu, 19th c. Bronze vajra, 15th c. Initiation card with vajras and mantra, 19th c. Offering vessel, 19th c)

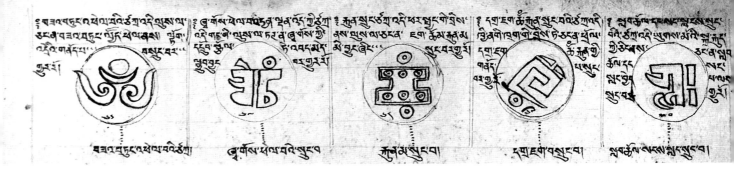

The medium

To produce an image is to make immediately present the spiritual principle it represents, and imbue a place or object with the energy of that principle. Each of the pieces shown here realizes its energies in a different way.

The sacred script and formalized design of charms written or woodblock printed on paper *(above)* make them effective. The compassionate Bodhisattva incised on the stone *(centre)* recognizes the physical presence of the stone as one more manifestation of Buddhist truth. The towering ceremonial offering made of coloured butter – a vital food in Tibet – is meant to honour the Buddhist Dharma, through which and to which it is made *(below)*. Its very impermanence – it will be burned the following day – is part of its meaning, demonstrating that all reality is transient.

The three-dimensionality of the sculptured figures illustrates how space itself is a function of the Buddha-mind. The huge modelled and painted image in the main shrine at Gyantse *(top right)* emerges from the fabric of the sacred building, to be a permanent revelation of indwelling Buddha-presence. It is honoured by the white silk scarves draped over it. The small bronze of a Mahāsiddha pointing to the earth is modelled as a continuum of rounded, containing volumes, which illustrate his indwelling energy and inner possession of all space. Originally it would have contained rolled-up paper strips with charms and coloured fabric.

The painting of the great teacher.
Padmasambhava *(right)* not only
illustrates his legendary life and
miracles, but is intended to make it
possible for a meditator who knows the
appropriate mantras to re-realize that
sacred and amazing phase of history,
not just in the two-dimensional picture,
but in full presence.

The strips of red and yellow cloth
which generally surround Tanka
paintings symbolize the rainbow 'door'
opening on to the open sky from which
the indwelling figures arrive. The lower
part of the dress will often have a
rectangular patch of fine figured silk
stitched in, symbolizing the paradisal
waters across which figures appear.
(Page from book of charms against
evils. Mani stone carved with the
Bodhisattva Avolakiteśvara. Butter-
sculpture, Dungkar monastery,
Chumbi. Buddha figure, Gyantse.
Mahāsiddha Avadhūtipā, bronze, 15th
c. Padmasavabhava, Tanka, 18th c)

Compassionate beings

The 'Bodhisattva' is a stage of being especially valued in northern Buddhism, and contrasted with the being known as Arhat or Lohan. The latter attains release from the cycles of existence by accumulating Karmic merit on a personal basis, while the Bodhisattva continually dedicates and transfers his or her own inexhaustible stock of merit to the benefit of suffering creatures in all the millions of universes. Bodhisattvas appear as incarnations of utmost compassion, acting in many various and strange ways for the good of other beings trapped in the cycles of suffering. Our Buddha Gautama before he attained Nirvana is referred to as the Bodhisattva, since in his previous existences he had acted always out of selfless compassion, and so had earned the right both to Nirvana and to teach the way towards it.

The best-known Bodhisattva is Avalokiteśvara, Tibetan Chen-re-zi, the 'Looking-down Lord' or 'Lord who gazes compassionately down upon the world'. Each Tulku Dalai Lama, head of the Gelugpa sect, is regarded as one of his incarnations. *Above*, the image of many-armed Avalokiteśvara can be seen behind his incarnation, the fourteenth Dalai Lama. Different versions of Avalokiteśvara have different numbers of arms. The Bodhisattva Manjūśrī, *far left*, also appears in various forms. His more common form appears at top left of the Tanka shown *below left*. The central figure of the Tanka is Vajrabhairava, 'Terrible Vajra', the same principle of compassion in fierce form. The fierce Bodhisattva Vajrapāṇi, 'Vajra-in-hand', *right*, represents the power of the Enlightened state.

Maitreya, *below, left and right*, is the Bodhisattva at present on the way to becoming the next incarnate Buddha. He is therefore at the stage of still living through his infinitely many lives of compassion. (Manjūśrī, bronze, 18th c. The Dalai Lama, contemporary photograph. Vajrabhairava, Tanka, 18th c. Vajrapāṇi, bronze, 16th c. Maitreya, bronze, 15th c, Tanka, 18th/19th c)

Female Sky-goers

Buddhism originated in a male-oriented Indian society which did not accept that Enlightenment was available directly to the life-phase 'woman', and turned so far away from sexuality that for a monk even to look at a woman in the face was forbidden. The true Vajrayāna Buddhism of northern India and Tibet, whose imagery is illustrated here, assimilated vital ancient – perhaps neolithic – traditions that survive still in India. Vajrayāna regards the desire to see oneself as 'pure', 'detached' and 'clever' as among the most difficult cravings to overcome and ultimately the most limiting. One of the greatest old Vajrayāna texts, the

Guhyasamāja, describes the Buddha teaching a horrified audience that no one is qualified for Enlightenment who has not broken, and seen themselves as breaking, every code of conventional 'decent' behaviour.

This belief combined in Vajrayāna with the ancient tradition that it is specially endowed women, not men, who are the vessels of primary creative and spiritual power; and that male yogis and meditators need to gain their initiation and spiritual potency by sexual intercourse. Tibetan tradition recounts such initiations of great founding saints of Vajrayāna Buddhism, Tilopa, for example.

Successful meditation depended on methods of sexual yoga.

Female 'power-holders' were often called Dākinīs, translated into Tibetan as Khadomas, 'Sky-goers'. *Top right*, Mahāsiddhas, 'great practitioners', are shown with their consort 'flying through the space of emptiness'.

The *yab-yum* imagery of sexual partnership in Vajrayāna Buddhism *(centre)* is interpreted as the union of 'method and wisdom'. The 'father' or male signifying 'skilful means' or active compassion is united with Wisdom or emptiness, the 'mother' or female signifying passive, intuitive knowledge of the illusory nature of creation.

At far right, the sexual exchange is illustrated by a bronze female figure

separated from a *yab-yum* statue still wearing her consort's sexual organs. The bone figure, *right*, is probably an offering goddess, dancing with a scarf to symbolize the sense of touch. (Naropa's Dākinī, detail of Tanka, *c.* 17th c; bronze of the same figure, 18th c. Initiation painting such as is used for the third or Wisdom initiation in Highest Yoga tantra, mounted as a Tanka, 18th c. Monk dancing in full dress as a Dākinī, contemporary photograph. Chakra Saṁvara in union with his consort Dākinī, bronze, 18th c. Flying Dākinī, detail of Tanka, 18th c. Bronze female figure, 18th c. Bone figure, front and rear views, *c.* 19th c)

Human teachers

The human teacher is venerated, and regarded as all-important in introducing the meaning of the Dharma to disciples and showing them the Path from experience. The deep respect accorded to the great unbroken line of teachers, extending from the Buddha

through the Tibetan translators and masters – the greatest of whom founded their own traditions – is indicated in the Tanka shown *left*. Here the founder of the Gulugpa sect, Tsongkapa, wearing his pointed hat, sits at the summit in the place usually given to the Supreme Buddha. The main central figures of the Tanka, Vajrasattva in union with his female Total Wisdom, symbolize the union of method and insight which constitutes the teaching. *Above* is portrayed a revered teacher, a lama who lived probably in the fifteenth century. The Tanka *above right* bears outlines drawn around the hands and feet of a venerated master, which impart to the piece his power and insight. The gilt headdress, *right*, when worn in meditation, transforms the person meditating into the very essence of the Dyhāni Buddhas: five around the rim, the sixth, Vajrasattva, at the pinnacle. The decoration symbolizes the indwelling power. (Tanka, 18th c. Bronze figure, *c.* 15th c. Tanka, late 19th c. Headdress, 19th c)

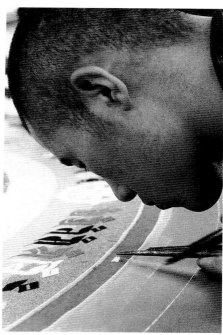

The design of Tankas and mandalas replicates traditional forms in order to provide temporary dwellings for divine principles. A mandala is a circular diagram of the process by which the cosmos unfolds from its centre, demonstrating its total internal coherence through causal interdependance, and the void nature of all apparently separated things. But Tibetans recognize that true mandalas can only ever be mental, and are vastly many. Physical images are convenient means for promoting true mandalas in people's minds, sacred only for the periods during which they are in service. The communal Kālachakra ceremony centres on a major mandala of which the monk *above right* is making a temporary diagram with coloured sands. The painted mandala diagrams, *left* and *opposite*, are meant as aids to building the mental mandalas needed in following-through meditative ritual texts. Some of these texts, like the *Śrichakrasambhāra*, consist almost entirely of instructions for mentally formulating and resolving series of interlinked mental mandalas, incorporating mantras as vital elements. (Painting a Tanka, making a sand-mandala, contemporary photographs. Detail of Mandala Tanka, 18th c. Tanka with mandalas, 18th c)

The meditative system

The Buddha-nature, the Dharmakāya, which the meditative system models, has three main aspects, *Kāya-Vak-Citta*, 'Body-Speech-Mind', all of which have to be realized. They correspond with the three inner mandala-levels which the meditator formulates. *Kāya* corresponds with the heart level of the Dhyāni Buddhas. It means 'body', in the sense of universal spatial body spread out by the Buddha regions through Skandhas, sense-realms, Elements and passions (see pages 29–30). *Vak* (throat level) means 'speech' in the sense of formulated ideas and connections, whose matrix is language, and manifests in the severe Knowledge-holders. *Citta* means 'mind' as the source of those turbulent twistings and turnings which generate phenomena, represented at head level by six tempestuous Herūkas and their consorts.

The Tanka *opposite* represents all three. At the centre are the violent Herūkas, surrounded by a circuit of terrifying apparitions like those in the dance-drama. The Knowledge-holders are at the bottom centre; four Dhyāni Buddhas sit within small circles, the fifth in the central axis above the Knowledge-holders, in place of Saṁvara. The guardians enveloped in flames are at the four quarters. At the top centre is Vadrahāra, and above again, remote and naked, the blue primordial Buddha, embraced by his white Wisdom, in whom all levels of Kāya-Vak-Citta are consummated. Down the sides are the six humane Buddhas who offer teaching in the six regions of the incarnation-cycle.

Certain sects worship variants of figures from this hierarchy. Among them are particular Dhyāni Buddhas, the guardian Yamāntaka as Raktayamāri, and Saṁvara as Kālachakra (Tibetan, Demchog). (Tanka of the Peaceful Dhyāni Buddhas, Knowledge-holders and Wrathful Buddhas, 18th c)

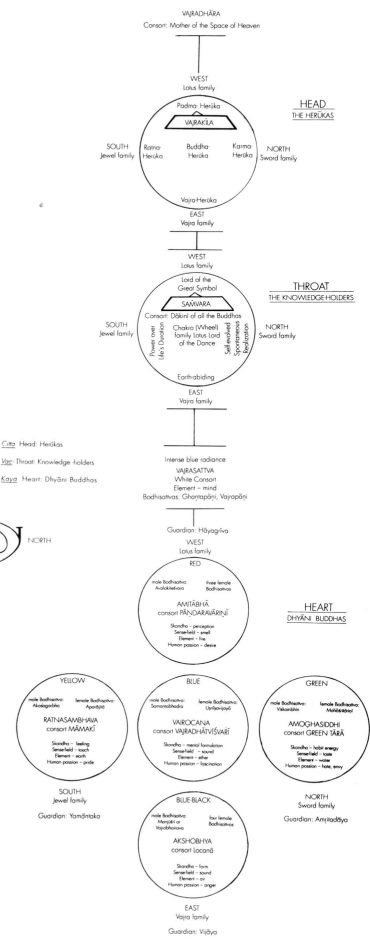

Transformation and transcendence

Art points towards the experience of transcendence through a series of transformative images. The Tanka, *left*, contains some of the imagery of the system displayed on the previous page, stressing the aspect of compassion, for the central figure represents the

supreme Bodhisattva Ghantapāṇi (Bell-in-hand). He is transformation of Vajrasattva, essence of all five Dhyāni Buddhas. Just below Ghantapāṇi is the fifth, focal, Dhyāni Buddha, Vairocana, in union with his consort; and around him the other four with their families. Along the lower edge are the five Knowledge-holders of the *Vak* (speech) region, while along the upper edge are ranged the six humane Buddhas who appear within the six regions of reincarnation, flanking the Supreme Buddha, blue-bodied Samantabhadra, united with his white consort. He is borne up beyond space and time by a small being who represents 'the Unimaginable' *(Acintya)*.

Guhyasamāja, 'Secret Assembly', with his consort, *below*, personifies the power of the Enlightened state and the transformation of anger into wisdom. The Bodhisattva of whom he is a transformation is the wrathful Vajrapāṇi, 'Vajra-in-hand', who appears as the chief figure in the Tanka at *lower left*, and again as the fierce figure in the small Tanka at *centre*.

Vajradhāra *(above)*, united in utmost tranquillity with his consort, 'Mother of the Space of Heaven', personifies the Dharmakāya, the Enlightened Mind. (Gantapāṇi, Tanka, 18th c. Vajrapāṇi, Tanka, 17th c. Dhyāni Buddha Akshobhya, represented here as the Supreme Buddha, with, *below*, his terrible form, Vajrapāṇi, embroidered Tanka, 19th c. Vajradhāra, bronze, 16th c. Guhyasāmaja, bronze, 17th c)

Select Bibliography

Bell, C., *The People of Tibet*, Oxford 1928.
——, *The Religion of Tibet*, Oxford 1931.
Bhattacharya, B., *The Indian Buddhist Iconography* (with *Sādhanamāla* translations), Oxford 1924.
Blofeld, J., *The Jewel in the Lotus*, Shanghai 1948.
Chang, C.C., *Teachings of Tibetan Yoga*, New York 1963.
Conze, E., *Buddhism*, Oxford 1957.
——, *Buddhist Thought in India*, London 1962.
Dasgupta, S.B., *An Introduction to Vajrayāna Buddhism*, Calcutta 1950.
David-Neel, A., *Initiations and Initiates in Tibet*, London 1931, 1950.
——, *With Mystics and Magicians in Tibet*, London 1931 (reissued as: *Magic and Mystery in Tibet*, New York 1971).
Essen, Gerd-Wolfgang, and Tsering Tashi Thingo, *Die Götter des Himalaya* (2 vols), Munich 1989. Descriptive catalogue of works in the Gerd-Wolfgang Essen Collection (Exhibition Cologne, Munich, Berlin 1989–90).
Evans-Wentz, W.Y., *The Tibetan Book of the Dead*, London 1927, 1957.
——, *The Tibetan Book of the Great Liberation*, London 1954.
——, *Tibet's Great Yogi Milarepa*, London 1957.
——, *Tibetan Yoga and Secret Doctrines*, Oxford 1935.
Fremantle, F., and Chögyam Trungpa, *The Tibetan Book of the Dead*, Berkeley 1975.
Govinda, Anagarika, *Foundations of Tibetan Mysticism*, London 1960, 1969.

——, *The Way of the White Clouds*, London 1966.
Guenther, H.V., *The Life and Teachings of Naropa*, London 1963.
——, *The Royal Song of Saraha*, Berkeley 1968.
Kazi-Dawa-Samdup (tr.), *Shrīchakrasambhāra Tantra*, ed. A. Avalon, London/Calcutta, 1919.
Krazinsky, P.C. van Korvin, *Die Tibetische Medizinsphilosophie*, Zurich 1953.
Murti, T.R.V., *The Central Philosophy of Buddhism*, London 1955, 1960.
Nebesky-Wojkowitz, R., *Oracles and Demons of Tibet*, The Hague 1956.
Pal, Pratapadita, *Art of Tibet*, Los Angeles County Museum of Art, University of California Press, Berkeley, Los Angeles, London, 1983.
Sierksma, F., *Tibet's Terrifying Deities*, The Hague 1966.
Snellgrove, D.L., *The Hevajra Tantra* (2 vols), London 1959
——, *Nine Ways of Bön*, London 1967.
——, with H. Richardson, *A Cultural History of Tibet*, London 1968.
Stcherbatsky, T., *Buddhist Logic*, Leningrad 1930, New York 1962.
Tucci, G. *Theory and Practise of the Mandala*, London 1961.
——, *Tibetan Painted Scrolls* (3 vols), Rome 1949.
Waddell, L.A., *The Buddhism of Tibet*, London 1895, Cambridge 1934.

Acknowledgments

I am glad to acknowledge the assistance of Brian Beresford, who read the text and made many helpful suggestions. Illustrations are acknowledged to the following collections and photographers (plate numbers in *italic* type, illustrations in the text and Themes sections indicated by page numbers with abbreviations: a above, b below, c centre, l left, r right):
Brian Beresford *10, 17, 25, 30, 65, 72b, 73l, 76al, 77a, 79a, 80a, 86r*; Martin Brauen *84ar*; Durham: The Oriental Museum, University of Durham *26, 27, 83br, 93*; Gerd-Wolfgang Essen *34, 16, 67, 68l, 74cr, 83l, 84b*; Collection Mr and Mrs John Gilmore Ford *22*; Werner Forman Archive/Philip Goldman Collection *7, 19, 35, 37, 95b*; Philip Goldman Collection *84al*; Ernst Haas *18*; Suzanne Held *11*; Archaeological Survey of India *66a*; C. Jest *71b, 77br, 81br, 90al*; Russell Johnson *4, 5, 15, 16, 20, 21, 33, 78bl, 79b*; Leiden: Rijkmuseum voor Volkenkunde *1, 9, 27*; London: British Museum *21, 75r, 76r, 85l*, Horniman Museum *80c*,

India Office Library (Bell Archive) *31, 18, 69a* (photo C. Claude White) *7, 70al*, Tibet Foundation *13, 71a*, Victoria and Albert Museum *23, 28, 4, 76bl, 80r, 82c, 85br, 87cr, 94a*; Lookat Photos/Manuel Bauer *12*; Los Angeles County Museum of Art (From the Nasli and Alice Heeramaneck Collection, Purchased with Funds Provided by the Jane and Justin Dart Foundation) *32*, (Julian C. Wright Bequest) *36*, (Gift of Christian Humann) *89l*; Fosco Maraini *3, 24, 68r, 74al, 74bl, 82b, 83ar*; Courtesy Ian Mills *19*; Ajit Mookerjee Collection *87l*; Paris: Galerie Marco Polo *20*, Musée de l'homme *69cl*, Musée Guimet *74br, 87a, 89ar*; Private Collection *14, 38, 69cr, 69b, 70r, 75l, 76c, 78r, 79c, 81al, 81ar, 81bl, 81c, 85a, 86b, 90b, 91, 95a*; Remote Source/John Batten Photo Travel *29*; H.E. Richardson *72a*; Rotterdam: Copyright Museum voor land en Volkenkunde *66r, 80bl*; Courtesy Routledge and Kegan Paul Ltd *38*; Edwin Smith *77l, 78a, 89l*; Office of Tibet, London *8, 73ar, 73cr, 73br*, Zurich *90r*; Zurich, Museum für Volkerkunde *70b*.